TAOISM

Descriptions and prescriptions for inner peace and beautiful living

Bill Barbic

Copyright © 2005 by Bill Barbic

All rights reserved. No part of this book shall be reproduced or transmitted in any form or by any means, electronic, mechanical, magnetic, photographic including photocopying, recording or by any information storage and retrieval system, without prior written permission of the publisher. No patent liability is assumed with respect to the use of the information contained herein. Although every precaution has been taken in the preparation of this book, the publisher and author assume no responsibility for errors or omissions. Neither is any liability assumed for damages resulting from the use of the information contained herein.

ISBN 0-7414-2772-9

Published by:

INFINITY
PUBLISHING.COM

1094 New DeHaven Street, Suite 100
West Conshohocken, PA 19428-2713
Info@buybooksontheweb.com
www.buybooksontheweb.com
Toll-free (877) BUY BOOK
Local Phone (610) 941-9999
Fax (610) 941-9959

Printed in the United States of America

Printed on Recycled Paper

Published September 2005

DEDICATION

This book is dedicated to my daughter Cassiopeia, who always believed in my work, but more importantly, always believed in me.

ACKNOWLEDGMENTS

I wish to thank Mr. & Mrs. Van Dyke for the considerable time and effort they put into copyediting this first book in the *Trilogy*. What a wonderful marriage of love and talent they are.

Because of the intricate and far-reaching connections between us all, I believe that every ancient and modern master, teacher, author, and practitioner of Taoism has, in some distant way, contributed to the creation of this work. So, I also wish to acknowledge my debt to them all.

CONTENTS

PREFACE 1
  WHY I WROTE THIS BOOK 1
    THE INTENT 1
    THE PROBLEM 1
    THE SOLUTION 2
  HOW I WROTE THIS BOOK 3
    THE FORMAT 3
    THE CONTENT 7
TAOISM 11
  INTRODUCTION TO TAOISM 11
    WHAT IS THE TAO? 11
    WHAT IS TAOISM? 12
    TAOISM and YOU 13
  TAOISM and RELIGION 15
    SECULARISM 15
    ECLECTICISM 17
    RATIONALISM 17
    THE SOURCE 18
  THE HISTORY OF TAOISM 18
    ORIGINS 18
    I CHING 19
    TAO TE CHING 21
    CHUANG TZU 28
    LIEH TZU or LIEZI 31
  THE PSYCHOLOGY OF TAOISM 34
    INTRODUCTION 34

INNER PEACE 35
OUTER PEACE 51
AWARENESS 58
NON-DUALITY 63
DETACHMENT 69
HAPPINESS 79
ENLIGHTENMENT 83
MEDITATION 87

THE PHILOSOPHY OF TAOISM – EPISTEMOLOGY 119
TRUTH 119

THE PHILOSOPHY OF TAOISM – ETHICS 124
PERSONAL RESPONSIBILITY 124
P'U (Authentic Being) 131
TZU-JAN (Authentic Living) 136
WU-WEI (Non-Doing) 149
ADAPTABILITY 166
SAN PAO (The Three Treasures) 172

THE PHILOSOPHY OF TAOISM - AESTHETICS 174
LI (Form or Organic Pattern) 174

THE PHILOSOPHY OF TAOISM – METAPHYSICS 176
INTRODUCTION 176
TAOIST COSMOLOGY 177
CH'ANG (Laws) 178
TE (Virtue Energy) 181
CHI or QI (Cosmic Energy) 183
YIN and *YANG* (Polarity) 190
I (Change) 202
WU-HSING (The Five Elements) 204
FENG SHUI (Wind and Water) 207

FU (Return) 261
WU (Non-Being) 263
NATURE 264
WHOLENESS 268
ONENESS 270
DIVINATION 278
PARADOX and MYSTICISM 285

ENVOI **288**
GLOSSARY **289**

PREFACE

WHY I WROTE THIS BOOK

THE INTENT

As indicated in the subtitle, my intent in writing this book is to provide the reader with descriptions and prescriptions for inner peace and beautiful living.

THE PROBLEM

Few of us living in this frenzied and troubled world need to be convinced of the need for more inner peace and beautiful living. Day after day, we put on our costume, select our mask, enter our stage of life, and feel the heat of the spotlights upon us. Amid our props, we deliver our lines with more and more anxiety and less and less enthusiasm. But we still hope for some friendly applause.

One day when the lights begin to dim, we see through our delusions. We have an epiphany. We realize that this is our life, but not entirely our script. We have been letting others select and direct our desultory performances. We have been smiling on the outside and crying on the inside. Our life is both a comedy and a tragedy. It indeed has been an *act*.

Now seeing with new eyes, we begin to end our soul-eroding denial. We stop our *great lie*. We vow to liberate ourselves from the empty, senseless artificiality of it all, and regain our authenticity... before the final curtain comes down.

THE SOLUTION

THE FEAST FROM THE EAST:

The Eastern world holds many of the answers that the Western world desperately seeks and urgently needs. East plus West is best.

The principles and practices that have helped millions of people for thousands of years in the East can now help us in the West in many ways. If we are just open to its wisdom, we can tame our demons, heal our wounds, balance our excesses, focus our attention, and achieve true inner peace and beautiful living.

And here is the good news: You do not have to give up or even compromise your existing beliefs. The philosophic and psychological dimensions of these three secular traditions do not inherently conflict with any religion. In fact, they can make you better at your present practice because they can make you better at who you are.

THE DYNAMIC DUO:

The great intellectual traditions of the East and the West can function alone. But they can also be so much more together. In fact, they really need each other. (Much like women and men, and *yin* and *yang*.) Each is like a good recipe that is missing some key ingredients from the other to become truly great. Once again, thesis + antithesis = synthesis.

By combining the Eastern emphasis on the inner world with the Western emphasis on the outer world, a very powerful synergy can be created. The intelligent blend of the best principles and practices from East and West has the potential to usher in a golden era in both worlds.

THE TRILOGY:

Is it possible to present three of the East's greatest belief systems in a way that is intelligible, useful, and even interesting? This has been my challenge for many years.

This is the first book in a trilogy on three great Eastern traditions. The second book is *Buddhism*, and the third *Zenism*. They are presented in the approximate order in which they historically evolved.

TAOISM:

In this book, we explore the Taoist way to inner peace and beautiful living. In its psychology we find the secrets of awareness, non-duality, detachment, and enlightenment. In its philosophy, we discover the treasures of epistemology, ethics, esthetics, and metaphysics.

HOW I WROTE THIS BOOK

THE FORMAT

TABLE OF CONTENTS:

The Table of Contents is more detailed than most to give the reader a comprehensive outline of the subject. So one can instantly see that the history of Taoism includes four foundation texts; that the psychology of Taoism includes non-duality and detachment; and that *wu-wei* and *Feng Shui* are part of the metaphysics.

HEADINGS:

Context is important for understanding. It is frustrating to read several paragraphs, or even pages, trying to find out what an author is attempting to say. So I have used headings and subheadings very frequently throughout this book in order to give the reader a framework to understand the text.

MODULARITY:

With a few exceptions, each subject stands alone. It is not necessary to have read all the preceding material to understand the message. Each principle or practice is presented as an individual lesson module. Like a box of chocolates, *Taoism* is a sampler of ideas and concepts to be tasted and enjoyed in bite-sized pieces.

DESCRIPTIONS AND PRESCRIPTIONS:

Each subject in *Taoism*, is presented in two-parts:

Part-1: "Descriptions" For Understanding:

"Descriptions" concisely conveys the essence of each essential Taoist principle and practice. This first part of each subject is my interpretation of the classical teachings. It is a clear, coherent look at the original, fundamental elements of this "ism." "Descriptions" contain the expository dimension of the book. The subjects are organized under the broad headings of psychology and philosophy. "Descriptions" pierce the Taoist veil of mysticism and inscrutability, and explain the original ideas of the founders as faithfully as possible i.e., without "spin."

As you read this first concept-rich section, please keep an open mind. Suspend immediate judgment. Remember that to improve your life, you must be receptive to ways to do so. You must see the world in a different way.

Read this distilled expository material as you would eat a rich desert – slowly and in small bites. Take time to savor and digest each bit of wisdom. Allow each to seep into the deeper levels of your mind. Speed-reading is not recommended.

Part-2: "Prescriptions" For Inner Peace and Beautiful Living:

The second "Prescriptions" part of each subject applies the Taoist principles and practices from "Descriptions" to contemporary life. Here the reader will find a set of simple recommendations and rhetorical questions formulated to achieve the overall goal of inner peace and beautiful living. This is the practical, "how to" dimension of the book. It suggests reader participation. But the effort can potentially yield an inestimable personal return on the reading investment.

Please take these prescriptions as they are intended: well-intentioned *suggestions*. Not all may apply to you. Not all have to. Don't argue with the page. Simply select the suggestions that do apply. Remember that they are all meant to help you. If the reader embraced the prescriptions in each subject, and methodically brought them into daily living, there is no hurt that could not be healed, nor potential that could not be actualized.

"Prescriptions" are usually not found in books on Eastern thought. They are holistic human development recommendations for the reader. They are based on my own, as well as many others, ideas and experiences. I have not taken this material from any particular *arhat*, *bodhisattva*, Buddha, guide, guru, *geshe*, lama, master, monk, nun, *rinpoche*, *roshi*, shaman, teacher, *yogi*, or yogin. However, I hope that these luminaries would concur with them.

Two Books in One:

This two-part format essentially creates both an expository textbook of descriptions, and a transformational self-help book of prescriptions.

QUOTATIONS:

Quotations are like flashes of lightning. They illuminate the terrain of a subject. A good quote has the ability to bring us a different perspective. It has the power to pierce to the truth of a matter and to inspire us toward ideals.

To illustrate that the same ideals exist in the human heart everywhere, and to add a small plank in the bridge between the East and West, I have used quotations from both sides of the Pacific Ocean like bookends on topics. Where appropriate, a quote from the East begins a topic, and a quote from the West appends it. My purpose in doing so is twofold: First, to help the reader quickly grasp the gestalt of the topic. Second, to demonstrate the commonality of thought between East and West despite the cultural differences.

LANGUAGE:

What the West knows of Taoism comes to us through translations of Chinese. So most, but not all, of the foreign words in this book are Chinese. For instance, *wu* is a key Chinese word meaning "non-being."

FONT AND BOXES:

Quotes and special words are italicized. Major headings and key thoughts are in bold. Notes and stories are in boxes.

GENDER:

Instead of being gender neutral by continually writing "he or she", at times I use "he" and other times "she." Let's hope a word count confirms an approximate equality of the sexes that mitigates any potential exclusion neurosis in either sex.

FIRST PERSON:

Disclosure is part of honesty. I used the first person "I" to indicate what originates with me, and to distinguish it from part of an established doctrine. For instance, in the subject on *Feng Shui*, I state:

"Based on my studies of Feng Shui, I believe the following three premises (3 C's) are the basis of its theory and practice:"

The "3 C's" listing is not, to the best of my knowledge, found in any Taoist teachings other than my own.

THE CONTENT

TRADITIONAL TAOIST TEACHINGS:

Long ago in Asia, students of Taoism learned by being around masters. They were apprentices of life. They observed the ways of the wise, and listened to their sage advice.

Many today still believe that it is necessary to have a teacher or spiritual guide to reach the higher levels of

Taoist insights. But in our modern world, especially in the West, Taoist masters are not on every street corner.

I encourage the serious student of Taoism to seek a teacher, guide, or master. But until you find one, and even after, read several books on Taoism written by authors with different perspectives.

POLYGENIC:

There are many excellent books on Taoism that are solely translations of the *Tao Te Ching*. They provide quotations, interpretations, and commentaries on each of its 81 sections.

This book takes a different approach. Although it includes many quotes and concepts from the *Tao Te Ching*, it is certainly not another translation of it. Rather, it is an outline of the original, essential principles and practices drawn from several classics.

AUTHENTICITY:

History:

In their epic exposition of civilization, historians Will and Ariel Durant concluded that history defies categorization and generalization. What we know about the past is suspect because our evidence is fragmentary, and questionable. Inferences are dicey, and generalizations always have exceptions. We must often rely on legends and myths that both contain and obscure the truth. Fictionalized accounts of reality abound. As the ever satirical Voltaire said: "*History is nothing but a pack of tricks which we play on the dead.*"

Originality vs. Embellishments:

Some interpretations of Taoism, Buddhism, and Zenism carry an authoritative aura when they are really opinionated commentaries that are far from the founder's original thoughts. Simple, universal, truths no longer stay simple when overzealous sectarian scholars become self-appointed spiritual messengers. With an authoritative mien, they practice a subtle historical revisionism by lavishly embellishing the original basic teachings with a pastiche of their own. They imaginatively decorate the original simple foundation structure with elaborate edifices to their liking, and mythologize the main players. Soon there are complex rules, needless formalities, endless erudition, serious sermonizing, authoritative dogma, elaborate systems, impressive pageantry, mysterious rituals, mind-stretching superstitions, supernatural feats, and miracle stories.

Cults and parochialism invariably develop which further complicate and radicalize the movement. The serious seeker must recognize these spiritual sophists, resist their intoxicating allure, and always come back to the founder's original teachings. So the reader of this book will not find the dramatic stories, secret practices, and magical powers of any fringe movement in Taoism.

Nevertheless, considering the long history of Taoism (as well as Buddhism and Zenism) it is notable how much consensus exists on their essential principles and practices.

This work focuses on the tree of knowledge, not on its ornaments. I have attempted to extract what I believe to be the principles and practices of each tradition as originally conceived by their founders. I took care to winnow out the many personal creations of the later writers and teachers of these three "isms.

OBJECTIVITY:

I believe it is impossible for any writer to say with great assurance that his or her works are purely objective and free from personalistic judgments. Our psycho-dynamics are too complex. We all struggle with the inherent problems of *perceptual readiness* (the tendency to accept what we believe) and *perceptual defense* (the tendency to reject what contradicts.)

Nevertheless, my intention in writing the trilogy was to replicate as truthfully as possible the essential *psychology* and *philosophy* (not the later religious dimensions) of Taoism, Buddhism, and Zenism.

I have been careful to discern, and authentically transmit, the *original thoughts* of the founders of these "isms." The organization, metaphors, and style are of course mine. The *Prescriptions* section of each subject will also reflect my values.

TAOISM

INTRODUCTION TO TAOISM

WHAT IS THE TAO?

As if to test our determination to find the truth, the Tao shrouds itself in mystery. It is difficult to fathom, much less to explain, its inscrutable nature. The Tao is enigmatic, paradoxical, and transcendent. Perhaps the closest we can come to describing the indescribable is this:

The Tao is the eternal, infinite, <u>intelligence</u> and <u>power</u> that created, governs, and animates the world and universe.

The Tao is also known as "The Way", "The One", "The Void", "Teaching", "The Mother of All Things", "*Wu-Chi*", and other mysterious metaphysical names.

The Tao is the inexhaustible, universal, source of all life and all things. It is invisible, undetectable, and formless yet it is complete and vital. Its power is certain. It is as impersonal and impartial as a scientific law, and acts spontaneously without premeditation. It levels all opposites and finds the correct way amid all extremes. It moves in a systolic and diastolic wave. And it leaves nothing undone.

The Tao is often equated with the wisdom of nature. Taoists seek to understand and harmonize with the Tao (nature's way). This means not struggling to change it, or not departing from its direction.

The Tao is not a simple thing to be isolated, put under a microscope, analyzed, neatly packaged, and described. It is not intellectually accessed by one of the senses. It is so integrally and mysteriously a part of everything that an understanding of it can only be approached with all of one's faculties and being.

WHAT IS TAOISM?

DESCRIBING THE INDESCRIBABLE:

In this context, Taoism (pronounced "dowism") is defined as follows:

Taoism is the principles and practices of that psychology and philosophy teaching harmony with the Tao.

Taoism can also be understood as the path of least resistance with the Tao. It embodies naturalness, simplicity, and wholeness.

THE WATERCOURSE:

Taoism is often referred to as "The Watercourse Way" because of its powerful, vitalizing, and flowing nature. Like a watercourse, the essence of the Tao is flow. To try to label the Tao, and therefore limit it, is to fail to understand its omnipresence. This truth is contained in the famous, often-quoted beginning of the *Tao Te Ching*: *"The Tao that can be told is not the eternal Tao."*

PURPOSE:

If Taoism has a purpose, it is to become one with the Tao. The way to this oneness, is not though instruction, faith, or even focused effort. The way is through openness, intuition, adaptation, and even non-action (See "*Wu-Wei*" under "Metaphysics"). Taoism gently guides us to be respectful of, and in sympathy with, nature. It peacefully brings us in harmony with the Tao through our own inner sense of emptiness, stillness, simplicity, and oneness.

TWO WORLDS:

We live in a *visible* world of matter and forms. So we are naturally preoccupied with things. But we also live in an *invisible* world of energy and laws. So we are less aware of them. Taoism is about intelligently understanding and cooperating with this second world as it animates and governs the first.

TAOISTS ALL:

The Tao permeates, underlies, and animates all things -including us. So we are all Taoists in that we all exist within its laws. We all arise from, live within, and dissolve back into its infinite intelligence.

TAOISM AND YOU

Taoism is *not* an abstract tradition relevant only to an esoteric group of academics specializing in Eastern studies. It is a clear lens, which when placed over the world, allows us all to finally see that which has been obscure. Nor is Taoism a purely cerebral matter. It is a way of action and non-action that brings inner peace and beautiful living. The "Prescriptions" part of each subject in this book explains how this can be achieved.

Here are just three examples of how Taoist concepts have practical applications:

- An understanding of the relentless cycles of *yin-yang* can allow you to see ahead, and even predict the next turn of things.

- The practice of *wu-wei* (non-doing) can substantially reduce conflicts in your personal and professional relationships.

- The art and science of *Feng Shui* can enhance the beauty and functionality of both your work and living spaces.

The Tao is the most natural of "isms." Be open to its wisdom, connect with its power, and in time you will...

- Become aware of, identify, and resolve the blocks and pathologies that have slowed and crippled you

- Interfere less with the natural flow of people and things

- Begin to distinguish the essential from the nonessential, and the correct path from the expedient one

- Start on the path of serious self-cultivation

- Integrate the splintered aspects of your self into a meaningful whole

- Develop an inner calm amid outer chaos

- Notice the ebb and flow of your mental, physical, and emotional states; the cycles of nature; and the endless creative process of *yin-yang* interaction

- Understand your true nature, and hidden potentials

- Develop a strong sense of balance, direction, discipline, self-confidence, and self-sufficiency.

- Find great joy in the simple things of life, and eliminate the need for programmed consumption and superficial appearances

- Develop a great reverence for, and compatibility with, the beauty and power of nature

- Find your sacred path in life, and eliminate long and wasteful detours and dead ends

TAOISM and RELIGION

SECULARISM

THIS BOOK:

This book is on classical *philosophical* Chinese Taoism based on the teachings of the authors highlighted in "The History of Taoism."

NON-RELIGIOUS:

The author/founders of philosophic Taoism did not set out to create a religion. Their writings do not refer to God, deities, or spiritual beings. Nor was philosophic Taoism organized around a prophet, central figure, or contemporary leader. In fact, there is no monolithic organization structure in Taoism.

It was slightly before the beginning of the Christian era that Taoism began to develop into an organized religion with priests, rituals, scriptures, and ceremonies. These aspects of Taoism in its latter development are not the subjects of this book.

BEYOND CONVENTION:

The reader should not assume that the secular nature of Taoism renders it amoral. On the contrary, it rises far above, and moves far beyond, the questionable, ever-changing, man-made, religious and governmental systems that often contradict each other. The Tao provides a beginning less, steady, and endless source of wisdom that transcends theological rules, laws, canons, rituals, commandments, and punishments.

NO MIDDLE MAN:

Rather that ask you to trust and obey a minister, priest, rabbi, cleric, or other religious figure, Taoism asks you to directly connect to what is true and good. Trust your own way to spiritual development. Why? Because the premise of Taoism is that we are not broken, tainted, sinful, or missing anything. There is no need to be "found", "redeemed", "saved", or "born again."

Taoism holds that there is a permanent, pure essence inside each of us - no matter how wrong or even evil we may have been.

If we are open to the Tao, that seed can be nurtured and can grow into greatness.

NOT PARTITIONED:

Western religions partition God from man. There is a distinct divide. There is God and far, far below in a completely different realm there is man.

In Christianity, the separation of God and man came early – in the Garden of Eden. We were expelled, and destined to life in this valley of tears. The idea of *original sin* furthered this divide, as well as countless other rules and rituals.

Taoists believe we are intrinsically endowed (or "en-Tao-ed") with the spirit. There are no intrinsic deficits or defects that we have to work on. We have a pure essential being within that is accessible. We only need to find what we already have.

ECLECTICISM

To be a Taoist, there is no formal training, vows, or initiations.

You do not have to join a monastery or visit a temple. Some Taoists are monastic, vegetarian, celibate, and very spiritual. Others are worldly, omnivorous, married, and materialistic. Each Taoist is a unique and independent transformation list tending to their spiritual development. Taoists never resort to intrusive proselytizing. Followers of the Tao recognize that there are many, diverse paths along *The Way*.

RATIONALISM

Not unlike modern scientists, Taoists observe and learn from nature. They employ rationalistic and intuitive methods to discern cause and effect. Over time, repetition reveals patterns. And from these patterns, develop natural laws. The simple way of nature becomes their guide. They see no need to create myths, supernatural beings, messengers, gurus, revelations, scriptures, prayers, rituals, sects, orders, rewards, punishments, temples, or structures. There are no raging, gesticulating, evangelists preaching with an arrogant hubris. No Taoist acts as though he has a hot line to Heaven. No Taoist claims to "know" what God is thinking and feeling, and "know" whom He will reward and punish.

THE SOURCE

Taoists believe that the Tao is the source of all things, and that all things return to their source (See *"Fu"* under "The Philosophy of Taoism – Metaphysics"). So they continually access the origin for guidance. This may mean simply being silent and still, and making room for the answer. They well understand what is so foreign to Western culture: that much can be accomplished through non-action and non-interference (See *"Wu-Wei"* under "The Philosophy of Taoism – Ethics"). They simply seek a tranquil oneness with the wisdom of the Tao.

THE HISTORY OF TAOISM

ORIGINS

INTRODUCTION:

Taoism evolved before Buddhism and Zenism, and greatly influenced the development of both. Along with Buddhism and Confucianism, Taoism has affected every area of Chinese life for thousands of years. With its simple focus on individual needs, and nature's imperatives, it resonates to this day, especially with the peasantry in their close association with land and climate.

Unlike other major belief systems, Taoism was not founded by one charismatic figure. It evolved from several sources over a considerable period of time. It began in China and spread to Japan and Asia general.

FOUNDATION TEXTS:

The exact origin of Taoism is unknown, but it seems to have taken root with the following four ancient books:

1. *I Ching* or *Chou-I: Book of Changes* by various authors

2. *Tao Te Ching* or *Daode Jing* (pronounced "dow deh jing") by Lao Tzu (pronounced "louw-ser")

3. *Chuang Tzu, Changtse,* or *Zhuangzi* (pronounced "jwang-ser") by an author of the same name

4. *Lieh Tzu,* or *Liezi* by an author of the same name

The authors of the second book, Lao Tzu, and the third, Chuang Tzu, are often viewed as the co-founders of philosophic Taoism.

These four seminal Taoist texts have spawned hundreds of interpretations and commentaries through the ages. Here is a brief overview of each:

I CHING

"When the way comes to an end, then change – having changed, you pass through." - I Ching

THE TITLE:

The first and oldest foundation text of Taoism is the *Chou-I* (old name) or *I Ching* (new name). *"I"* means "change" or "transformation." *"Ching"* means book, sacred book, Toa, and truth. Therefore the *I Ching* is known as the *Book of Changes* or *Sacred Book of Changes*. This ancient text of wisdom has been credited with being the origin of two of China's most enduring belief systems – Taoism and Confucianism.

19

THE AUTHORS:

The *I Ching* began to develop when China was transitioning from the Yin to the Chou Dynasty. The literature usually identifies three authors:

Fu His is recognized as the most important contributor to the *I Ching*. He was the first of China's three noble emperors who ruled somewhere at the start of Chinese history - between 2900 and 2700 BC.

King Wen is the second contributor who was one of the founders of the Chou Dynasty, which lasted from 1111 to 249 BC. Some believe that he developed the 64-gua or hexagrams (two trigrams) divination method of the *I Ching* using the ideas of the unity of nature, and the equivalence of meaning.

A third contributor on record is the Duke of Chou (Zhou)

K'ung Tzu (Confucius) reportedly added narrative to this venerable work, though this in dispute. The *I Ching* eventually became one of the five Confucian classics.

THE BOOK:

Significance:

The *I Ching* is an essential part of Taoism. It has shaped Chinese culture for over two millennia in the following three ways:

Philosophy:

The *I Ching* provides moral guidance through the ethical structure in its philosophy.

Art:

The elegantly simple hexagrams and beautifully flowing Chinese characters within the *I Ching* is high art.

Oracle:

The *I Ching* offers oracular guidance. (See "Divination" under "Metaphysics.") It does so through a system of solid (*yang*) and broken (*yin*) lines that form trigrams and hexagrams with symbolic meaning. This divination aspect of the *I Ching* is one of the primary reasons it has maintained its popularity for so many centuries.

(From the West: "*I believe that the future is only the past again, entered through another gate.*" – Arthur Wing Pinero)

TAO TE CHING

"*The Tao that can be told is not the eternal Tao. The name that can be named is not the eternal Name.*" – Lao Tzu

THE TITLE:

The second foundation text of Taoism is the elegantly crafted *Tao Te Ching*. Let's examine each word in this name:

Tao means the way, the road, or the course. This metaphor refers to the divine path of the world and cosmos.

Te or *Teh* (See "*Te*" under "Metaphysics") means virtue or character of the purest kind – that which is unaware of its own quality. Those who possess *Te* live genuinely. They are graceful, virtuous, creative, dynamic, and unencumbered by internal conflict. They harmonize with their time and place, think clearly and decisively, and act efficiently and effectively.

Ching means sacred book. Other interpretations are: *The Book of the Impermanence of the Way* or *The Classic of the Way and its Power*, or to be brief, *The Book of the Way*.

Lao Tzu, the author, reportedly chose the word *Tao* in the title out of convenience. The book was originally referred to by the author's name. It was later given its present name by the emperor of the Han Dynasty. He elevated its status to that of a Confucian Classic by using the word "*Ching*" in the title.

THE AUTHOR:

Uncertainties:

Most historians believe Lao Tzu (a.k.a. Lao Tsu, Laotse, Li Erh and Lao Tan) is the author of the *Tao Te Ching*. His name means "Old Master." However, some historians believe he lived before the *Tao Te Ching* was written. Even if this were true, he is still considered to be its spiritual author because of his profound influence on Taoist thinking.

His Life:

There is much controversy about the life of the enigmatic and owlish Lao Tzu. Some believe that Lao-tzu never existed, and that the *Tao Te Ching* is a collection of teachings from various sources. What is myth and what is truth becomes obscure over time. As the great historian Will Durant reminded us, much of history is guessing.

Lao Tzu was born about 571 B.C.E. (Before Christian

Era). We know little about his youth of Lao Tzu. He spent his middle years in the Chinese Imperial Capital of Loyang. He held the position of Palace Secretary, and later Chief of the Imperial Archives at the Court of Chou. This latter position, which he held for a long time, allowed him to access the classic texts of his time.

Lao Tzu married and had a son named Tsung who became a soldier. He loved simple country folks of good will, and felt a great affinity with nature. Despite his high position, he was more a rusticator, preferring country living. He lived quietly and peaceably.

Lao Tzu and Confucius:

Many texts on Taoism describe a meeting between Lao Tzu and Confucius. Confucius, perhaps as much as 50 years younger than Lao Tzu, sought advice from him on proper behavior. Lao Tzu reportedly admonished Confucius over his preoccupation with useless and artificial formalities and appearing wise or wealthy. He said to simply be true to the authentic self. After the meeting, history records that Confucius considered Lao Tzu to be a "dragon-like sage."

Confucius evolved into the traditional, practical, "official" philosopher of China who represented rationality, duty and responsibility. He had ambitions. Lao Tzu was the more untraditional, intuitive, lyrical, wandering mystic of China. He focused on nature, spirituality and deeper meanings. He advocated "non-doing" (See "*Wu-Wei*" under "Ethics"). The reader might be tempted to choose between these quintessential left-right brain exemplars. A much better choice might be to respect the contributions of each, and benefit from the synergy of the combination.

Departure:

Lao Tzu did not preside over a school, but was nevertheless popular with students. One version of Lao Tzu's life includes his departure from his position, and society in general. He eventually became saddened by the decay of character in his time and grew tired of the court disputes. He realized that the seeds of his thoughts could not take root in the ground he lived on. So he resigned his revered position, left the Middle Kingdom, and rode west through the Han-Ku Pass.

Yin His and The Creation of The *Tao Te Ching*:

Yin Hsi, Guardian of the Mountain Pass, recognized Lao Tzu on his trek in northwestern China. He persuaded Lao Tzu to write down his thoughts for posterity before leaving the region. Little did this simple gatekeeper know that he would become the catalyst for what was to be one of the most influential books in world history.

Legend tells that Lao Tzu worked through the night to complete his masterpiece, and then departed in the morning.

Yin Hsi was so inspired by what Lao Tzu wrote that he gave up his position to follow him. Yin Hsi reportedly eventually became an important Taoist scholar, lived as a recluse, and disappeared into history.

Onward:

After the "Sage of the Page" put down his pen, he continued his journey West to India, where he is said to have met and perhaps instructed the Buddha (563 – 483 B.C.E.). One story even holds that these two giants of Eastern history were one and the same person!

THE BOOK:

Intent:

The Tao Te Ching was initially intended as a guide for leaders. However, in order to govern well, one must live well. So Lao Tzu's teachings enhance the art of living as well as the art of state governance. His timeless insights and practical advice have attracted readers from every socio-economic level in every era. He summarizes his teachings in Chapter 67 of the *Tao Te Ching* as follows:

"I have just three things to teach: simplicity, patience, and compassion. These three are your greatest treasures. Simple in actions and in thoughts, you return to the source of being. Patient with both friends and enemies, you accord with the way things are. Compassionate toward yourself, you reconcile all beings in the world."

Structure:

The *Tao Te Ching* contains 81 chapters and about 5000 words. (The number 81 is the square of the spiritually powerful number nine and the fourth power of the sacred number three.)

Popularity and Translations:

Some estimates are that the *Tao Te Ching* has been translated into English more than any other book except the Bible. There are many dozens of versions. This might seem puzzling. How could one book be interpreted differently so often? The answer may have much to do with the enigmatic writing style of the deeply mystical Lao Tzu. However different the wording of the various translations, the essence of each of the 81 passages should remain essentially the same. Choose the one that fits your cognitive predilections.

Themes:

What follows are some of the main themes of the *Tao Te Ching*. In the ripple affect of seminal historical events, several of them reappear in slightly different dress in Buddhism and Zenism.

Two Principle Themes:

The two principle subjects of the *Tao Te Ching* are the Tao and *Te* (virtue energy or the power of character). Of the 81 crisp epigrams of the *Tao Te Ching*, the first 37 are *The Book of the Way* (Tao). The next 44 are *The Book of the Te*. Before we part from our brief visit with Lao Tzu, here are some of the major thoughts from his masterpiece:

The Tao:

All things arise, are guided, and sustained by a mysterious, eternal, infinite, intelligence and power called the Tao.

Opposites:

Opposing qualities define and compliment each another.

Cycles and Return:

All things cycle and return to their essential nature. All things that have a beginning have an ending.

Modesty:

Avoids artifice and public displays. Keep a low profile, step aside, lets others go first, and remain humble. (How unlike our modern narcissistic culture.)

Thinking:

Do not myopically adhere to ridged dogma and senseless tradition. Be ever mindful of the dynamics of change, and of the resulting need to reassess situations. Be flexible and creative in thinking.

Acting:

Never cause more harm than good by forcing. Obey the principle of *wu-wei* or non-action. Be so at one with natural law that you are effortlessly efficient and effective. Act spontaneously and appropriately to the situation. (Very Zen.)

Conflict:

The most intelligent response to adversity is not battle or even resistance but avoidance.

The *Tao Te Ching* contains no references to God or to an afterlife. However, many passages sound biblical. Here are just a few excerpts that may have a familiar ring to Christians:

On Charity:

"*Before receiving, there must be giving.*" - Chapter 36

On Gaining The World And Losing The Soul:

"*Fame or self: Which matters more? Self or wealth: Which is more precious?*" - Chapter 44

On Adversaries:

"*Reward bitterness with care.*" - Chapter 63

(From the West: "*Nature is that which no man can define.*" – Elbert Hubbard)

CHUANG TZU

"Tao is beyond words. And beyond things. It is not expressed either in words or in silence. Where there is no longer word or silence Tao is apprehended." – Chuang Tzu

THE NAME / AUTHOR:

His Life:

The third foundation text of Taoism is the *Chuang Tzu* or *Zhuangzi* (pronounced "Jwahng-zer"). This text was named after the author and Chinese sage (approx. 369-286 B.C.E.).

Lao Tzu had a fertilizing influence on the thoughts and writings of Chuang Tzu (Chuang-Chou or Zhuangzi) who was his greatest disciple. Of course he had that influence on many people throughout history. Chuang Tzu further developed and explained many of the notions contained in the *Tao Te Ching*.

Like Lao Tzu, we do not know much for certain about the life of Chuang Tzu. So what follows is somewhat speculative. What seems certain is that he was one of the most spiritual of the Chinese philosophers. He may have come from the Meng District of China near what is now Henan (Ho-Nan) Province. He married, and held a minor administrative position.

Independence:

Chuang Tzu did not accept the traditional schools of Chinese thought of his time. He especially criticized (some say mocked) Confucianism. He considered its formality artificial and its ideas ungrounded in reality. (More thoughts that gave birth to the razor-sharp practice of Zen.)

Self-Realization:

Chuang Tzu believed that the greatest good was to live in accordance with one's true nature. (See "*P'u*" under "Ethics.") This idea was to be become famous in the West with Aristotle's (384 - 322 B.C.) philosophy of *self-realization*. This intellectual harmonic convergence, like so many others, testifies to the universality of truth. Truth has a habit of transcending time and space to reappear in different disguises in diverse cultures and eras.

Governance:

Chuang Tzu's spirit rebelled against an imposed and intrusive one-size-fits-all approach to governance. He believed bureaucratic reductionism does more harm than good. Chuang Tzu criticized institutions and governments for not staying out of the affairs of its citizens. He believed that the state should enact and enforce only a minimum of laws. In general, the state should maintain a hands-off, laissez faire approach to governance. (Note the similarity to the basic tenants of the modern Libertarian Party.) The people should be given the greatest possible freedom of choice because they, not the state, know what is best for them. Let the people take the path best suited to their own natures and conditions; needs and wants; talents and limitations. Only with the greatest freedom can they develop to their fullest in accordance with their natural abilities.

Change:

Chuang Tzu emphasized understanding the transient nature of the world. He considered nature to be a continuous flow of change. (In yet another example of common truth, Buddha had previously developed this same idea in the concept of *anicca* or impermanence.)

THE BOOK:

Chuang Tzu is both a commentary on Lao Tzu's *Tao Te Ching*, and an independent work. It has its own unique perspectives and themes. The early chapters are by the master. The later ones are by his disciples.

Along with other literary works, the *Chuang Tzu* text set in motion the intellectual forces that evolved into *Ch'an* in China (known as Zen in Japan).

The *Chuang Tzu* has been translated into English, French, and German. Considering the difficulty of understanding Chinese characters, and the challenges of reading the mind of this sage, any differences in the various interpretations are understandable and forgivable.

THEMES:

What follows below are some snippets describing the major themes in *Chuang Tzu*:

Change:

The world is in a constant state of transformation *(1)*.

Perspective:

Our individual perspective conditions our interprettation of the world. As our perspective keeps changing and maturing, so does our worldview. Therefore, we must stay flexible and not become locked into ridged dogmas and systems.

Independent View:

For clear view and correct response, we cannot be tied to fixed conventions that may or may not be appropriate for the situation.

Futility of Dispute:

The "right" and "wrong" of an issue cannot be determined through philosophic disputes.

Death:

It is both natural and inevitable that we all are going to die, so it is senseless to fear death.

LAO TZU AND CHUANG TZU:

Lao Tzu together with Chuang Tzu developed the philosophic core of Taoism. But their style and emphasis of writing are quite different. The intuitive, naturalistic Lao Tzu wrote short aphorisms that stir the heart. The practical, individualistic Chuang Tzu wrote long essays that stimulate the intellect and sense of humor.

Lao Tzu teaches acquiescence, humility, and the tactical advantage of keeping low to the ground like water. (*"Never be the first of the world."*) Chuang Tzu teaches skepticism of authority, non-conformity, and in general, a more recalcitrant approach.

Once again, we see *yin* (Lao Tzu) and *yang* (Chuang Tzu) working together. Synthesis, and antithesis combine to create thesis. Both of these pillars of Taoism agree on the wisdom of multiple perspective, adaptability, and naturalness in everyday living.

(From the West: *"Words are an unnecessary stain on silence and nothingness."* – Samual Beckett)

LIEH TZU OR LIEZI

THE NAME / AUTHOR:

The fourth foundation text of Taoism is the *Lieh Tzu* or

Liezi attached with an author of the same name. As with the previous sages, what we know about *Lieh Tzu* is fragmentary and suspect. He may have lived in the State of Zheng (Cheng) China, and he may have died in the fifth or even the fourth century B.C.E.

Modern scholars believe that Lieh Tzu existed, but are skeptical about his authorship. They believe the text bearing his name and thoughts was written around 300 A.D. by his followers long after his death. Perhaps we can assume, as we did with the thousand volumes attributed to Aristotle, that Lieh Tzu was not the literal author, but the inspiration behind the authors.

THE BOOK:

Themes:

The *Lieh Tzu* work is more coherent than the biography of its author. Its eight chapters deal with traditional Taoist themes such as the following:

Tao-Living:

Follow the Tao. This is not a matter of being scholastic and ritualistic. It is a matter of being open, intuitive, and harmonious.

Anti-intellectualism:

Be wary of dogmas, doctrines, and disciplines. Mistrust any elaborate, man-made, schemes to run our life or the universe. Man is not smart enough. Nature is. If we are at one with the Tao, our actions will be without calculating, or worrying. They will unconsciously and smoothly flow with the natural course of things always to good effect.

Illusion:

Be aware of your illusions. Life is a real phenomenon, but we experience it as an illusion i.e., we live in a "real dream." (This is a fundamental Buddhist concept.) Of course, most of us feel we are in touch with reality. But what reality is ours? Many of us feel we "know" the truth. But is it a universal truth we know, or a partial subjective one?

Synergy of Opposites:

Understand the necessity and usefulness of opposing forces. Opposites of all types are interconnected and mutually supporting. Opposing pairs of muscles in the human body perform voluntary movements. Prime movers and synergists contract while antagonists relax. We could not move if this dynamic duo did not oppose each other that way. The endocrine system both increases and decreases blood fluid, glucose, and electrolytes. In some cases, opposites actually define each other. (If there were no "up", there would be no "down.")

Altruism:

Lieh Tzu stressed the virtue of helping others. This is one of the Buddhist *Paramitas* or six perfections. (This is also one of the Christian values in the trio of faith, hope, and charity.)

Determinism:

The Chinese in general, and Lieh Tzu in particular, place great importance on determinism and a corresponding attitude of acceptance. (Very un-Western.) There is much in life that we do not control. Our options are to struggle with the inevitable (such as aging) or accept it and make the best of it.

Lieh Tzu taught that we should be in partnership with

the universe, not at war with it. Each of us has a certain destiny. The wisest course is not to fight it, but to live in harmony with it. We should not struggle with, and complain about, what we encounter on our path. Rather, we should naturally respond to what arises in the most appropriate manner, and flow with the inevitable. We should understand that what we think we engineered, was mostly our destiny all along. (The Chinese place a great deal of importance on fate.)

Life and Death:

Life and death are natural, inevitable, and interdependent, so we should not cling to the former or fear the latter. The idea is to understand and accept the cycle of life and death. We do not know what happens after death, so why worry about it? Besides, since life is such a struggle, death may be a relief and even a well-earned rest. Finally, we must apply this perspective not only to our life, but to others as well, especially those we love. No one will always be with us. Everything that has a beginning has an ending.

THE PSYCHOLOGY OF TAOISM

INTRODUCTION

After the foregoing brief review of the history of Taoism, we will now begin to explore the psychology of Taoism.

Here is a reminder of the format of each topic: Part-1: "Descriptions" explains the principles and practices of each of the essential elements of Taoism. Part-2: "Prescriptions" suggests how to benefit from them.

We will start with the first overall goal of this book as set forth in the subtitle - inner peace. With inner peace, every day becomes a joy. Without it, every day is a struggle.

INNER PEACE

"If my heart can become pure and simple like that of a child, I think there probably can be no greater happiness than this." – Kitaro Nishida

DESCRIPTIONS:

THE HIDDEN NEED:

It is difficult to find any ancient or modern teaching on wisdom that does not include the quality of inner peace. Any concept of success seems empty without it. But inner peace is like water, food, and money. We don't think much about it until it is missing. Then it becomes a high priority.

Inner peace is a hidden need, and therefore a neglected one. As individuals, we seem to forget its importance, and slowly suffer from its absence. As a society, we relegate it to a quaint sidebar of nice-to-do things. We suffer with our inner demons and difficulties, and charge forward with our ambitious agendas.

RECOGNITION:

Taoists observe the turmoil and tragedy of those who neglect inner peace. They witness the worship of the false gods of power, fame, and fortune. They marvel at the frenetic, soul-eroding pursuit of position, popularity, and possessions. They see others realizing at the end of their life - when it is too late - that they have sacrificed what was important for what was unimportant.

Taoists are ever mindful of the great necessity of inner peace. They know that there can be no lasting happiness or true success without it.

PERSONAL RESPONSIBILITY:

Taoists do not rely on others to bring them inner peace. They feel personally responsible for the creation and maintenance of inner peace in their life. They know that no one else can do this for them. (See "Personal Responsibility under "Ethics.") This position is self-empowering, and eliminates the tendency to blame others.

BEGIN WITHIN:

Taoists (as well as Buddhists and Zenists) begin all personal improvement within.

The Taoist way to inner peace is to not ignore or cover up problems by indulging in sensuous pleasures. He knows that diversions are never solutions, just as drugs may palliate symptoms, but not cure diseases. No matter how pleasant diversions in the outer world may be, he still has to come back to his inner world. When the high of drink, food, sex, drugs, entertainment, and conspicuous consumption wears off (as it always does), he still has to face his problems once again.

Taoists know that if the inner world isn't right, nothing else matters. They know that if you can't find inner peace inside, you won't find it anywhere else.

A HOLISTIC APPROACH:

The Taoists way to inner peace is holistic. The mind, body, and emotions must all be right. You cannot be at peace if your mind is troubled, your body is unhealthy, and your emotions are out of control. Lets examine these three dimensions of the self in the context of inner peace:

1. COGNITIVE CONTROL:

Taoists know that inner peace requires cognitive control. They understand that our mind is an ever-flowing stream of thoughts, which cannot be stopped, but can be channeled. They know that if we do not control our thoughts that the outside world will. And we may not like it takes us.

We cognize or experience all phenomena through the filters of our senses and through the processes of our mind. Our mind is the final arbiter of the significance of our reality. So awareness, discipline, and cognitive control are essential.

Taoists manage their mind to avoid thoughts that generate harmful emotions, and self-nullifying behavior. They listen to the subtle inner voice of their authentic being, and observe the peaceful way of the Tao.

2. NATURAL HEALTH:

Self-Sufficiency:

Taoists know that wellness contributes to inner peace. So physical health is important. Here again, they take personal responsibility. They do not abuse their body for years and then expect a costly, high-tech, medical-pharmaceutical complex to save them.

Taoists avoid that which erodes health, and embrace that which enhances it. They breathe, drink, eat, and live in accord with the principles of natural health.

Listening:

Taoists are open to the subtle messages that their body sends. They listen as their body communicates its needs and problems. They do not block out physical issues with denial, delusion, alcohol, or drugs. They sense what their body systems are trying to tell them. They respond in a timely, appropriate, and naturalistic manner.

Yin-Yang:

In the way of *yin-yang* (See "*Yin-Yang*" under "Metaphysics"), Taoists avoid excesses and deficits. They achieve balance and maintain anatomical homeostasis. This means getting the proper quantity and quality of sleep, exercise, fluids, and nutrients.

Not Forcing:

In the way of *wu-wei* (See "*Wu-Wei*" under "Ethics") Taoists do not force their body in any unnatural ways. This may seem obvious, but how often is this basic principle violated in the Western world? Westerners are known for forcing their bodies to work too much, play too much, drink too much, and of course eat too much.

3. EMOTIONAL WELL-BEING:

Taoists know that to have inner peace they must be in control their emotions. They understand the simple but important dynamic that thoughts drive feelings, and feelings can distort rationality.

Irrationality leads to rash behavior that creates unintended and unfortunate consequences. So Taoists monitor their feelings to make sure that they never become unhealthy or destructive.

TE:

How can one attain true inner peace while at war with the world? There is a saying in spiritual circles that captures this fundamental correspondence across the great boundary of existence: "*As it is within, so it is without.*"

Purity of intentions brings courage and strength.

Taoists ensure inner peace by developing greater *Te,* or virtuous character. With a strong inner world, they are better able to defend themselves from the relentless challenges of the outer world.

HARMONY:

The Taoist way to inner peace is to live in harmony with the teachings of the Tao. Nothing else is necessary, and anything else is a burden, which leads to the next principle of inner peace - simplicity.

SIMPLICITY:

For Taoists, simplicity is essential to inner peace. Ever growing clutter and complexity only lead to a troubled mind and heart. Clutter also blocks the free flow of *chi.* (See "*Fung Shui*" under "Metaphysics.")

Like the rest of nature's creations, Taoists need little to live well. Unlike many Westerners, they know the meaning of the word "enough." They know that they are secure in proportion to what they can do without.

APPRECIATION:

Instead of waiting for the one right day in the future when they have it all, Taoists take time to reflect on what is beautiful before them now. They do not need a medical crisis to learn to appreciate each moment of life for what it is. (This spirit is captured in the Zen concepts of *Sa-Be* and *Wa-Be*.)

WESTERN PSYCHOLOGY:

In investigating and eliminating any mental/emotional afflictions you may harbor, it may be helpful to become familiar with the main approaches in Western therapeutic psychology. What follows is a brief overview of four major schools:

- Psychoanalytic Analysis
- Behavioral Analysis
- Developmental Analysis
- Cognitive Analysis

PSYCHOANALYTIC ANALYSIS:

Introduction:

Psychoanalytic theory analyzes the unconscious, and often irrational, drives and motives that condition every aspect of a person's thoughts and behavior.

Two figures are prominent in the development of the field of psychoanalysis. They are: Sigmund Freud (1856-1939) and Carl Jung (1875-1961).

Sigmund Freud:

Sigmund Freud is considered the founder of modern psychoanalysis and one of the most influential thinkers of the 20th century. He was born in Austria, and became an M.D. who specialized in neurology. He believed that the mind was mostly unconscious. In this subterranean world, we keep our demons at bay. Freud emphasized the importance of five childhood stages centered on physical pleasure centers. Freud also postulated a three-part structure of personality consisting of the following:

The *Id*:

The *id* is the hedonistic, impulsive, self-gratifying child of the personality. It is energetic, instinctual, and sexual, and functions on the *pleasure principle* – seek pleasure and avoid pain. The primitive, impulsive *id* is not ready for prime time. It has no public contact with the conscious mind. It lurks in the shadowy, netherworld of the subconscious.

The *Superego:*

The *superego* is the idealistic, conscious-based, "high priest" of the personality. It holds the moral high ground. Like the ego, the operation of the superego is mostly hidden, but somewhat apparent to the conscious. The *superego* strictly judges right and wrong, but it fails to temper these judgments with reality. It is the *ego* that must counterbalance the *superego*'s idealistic ambitions with the realities of the real world.

The *Ego*:

The *ego* is the rational, realistic, adjudicating, manager of the personality. The *ego* strives for a middle ground between the reckless impulses of the *id* and the strict moral authority of the *superego*. A healthy *ego* abides by the *reality principle*, and acts as a wise moderator. An unhealthy *ego* will distort reality as a defense mechanism to protect itself from anxiety thereby producing a cognitive dissonance or tension. Though mostly submerged, some degree of the *ego* enters conscious thought.

Freud's construction of personality has been the subject of much debate and controversy. Regardless of the accuracy of the details of his conception, it seems reasonable that the intrinsic nature of these three aspects of the personality exist to some degree in all of us.

Carl Gustav Jung:

Carl Jung (1875–1961) was a contemporary of Freud who greatly extended the emphasis and importance of the subconscious mind. Among Jung's significant and several contributions to the field of psychoanalysis were the following:

The *Collective Unconscious:*

This is a repository of the experiences of mankind residing at the deepest level of the unconscious.

Archetypes:

These are the meaningful symbols or images residing in the collective unconscious that are common to everyone. Among the most prominent are the *anima* ("feminine" side of a man), the *animus* ("masculine" side of a woman), and the *shadow* (the immoral, evil, dark self).

Synchronicity:

This fascinating phenomenon is called "meaningful coincidence." It refers to a situation that arises when an image emerges from the unconscious into the conscious, and an event occurs in reality that is similar but not causally related.

Jung as well as Freud also studied the meaning of dreams. They both believed them to be symbolic of our subconscious conflicts.

BEHAVIORAL ANALYSIS:

Burrhus Frederick (B.F.) Skinner is generally recognized as the pioneer in the field of behavioral analysis. Skinner did not delve into the dark world of the unconscious. Instead he focused on modifying behavior that was observable, and developed the methods of "operant conditioning." In brief, he reinforcement desired behavior through rewards, and discouragement undesirable behavior through punishment to thereby condition an "operant" or behavior in a person or animal. (Not unlike Pavlov's conditioned responses.)

DEVELOPMENTAL ANALYSIS:

This approach investigates the lifetime history of the development of the individual to determine the nature of the pathology. In the extreme, it can start with an inquiry into past lives, but usually focuses on childhood. Much of what we are is determined by those early years. As Sigmund Freud said: "*Childhood determines.*" The developmental approach first identifies the problem, and then attempts to neutralize it with an association. Hypnosis is sometimes used to facilitate the process.

COGNITIVE ANALYSIS:

The First Cognitive Therapist?

Shakyamuni Buddha (a.k.a. Siddhartha Gautama) seems to have been the first in recorded history to articulate the principles of what we now call "cognitive behavioral therapy" or "rational emotive behavior therapy."

A close study of Buddha's original teachings indicates that he did not intend to establish a religion, but rather a philosophical and psychological system. His lifelong mission was essentially to end suffering through psychological health.

Since Buddha's time, cognitive analysis has had many diverse incarnations, contributors, and adherents. Greek philosophy - especially the stoical school - deals with the power of our thought to shape our life and the world.

Cognitive Control in a Nutshell:

Below in bold is the basic syllogism of cognitive control. To master this is to ensure your emotional well being for the rest of your life. It is so simple most people do not grasp how important and powerful it is.

We always seem to want something more complex and even technical. As you read this, think of how your mind works and test it for yourself.

Feelings are generated by thoughts. We can control our thoughts. Therefore, we can control our feelings.

We can trace an unhealthy feeling to an unhealthy thought. Correct the thought and feel better. It is that easy. Though negative thoughts can arise in your mind automatically, you do not have to entertain them. You do not have to add to them and torture yourself with them. Recognize them for what they are when then enter. Then just let them pass. And they will if you do not grasp on to them. Use displacement. The mind cannot hold two thoughts at once. Substitute a good, healthy thought for one that is a vexation to your spirit.

(From the West: "*The wise man seeks not pleasure, but freedom from care and pain.*" – Schopenhauer)

PRESCRIPTIONS:

"The pure men of old acted without calculation, not seeking to secure results. They laid no plans. Therefore failing, they had no cause for regret; succeeding, no cause for congratulation." – Chuang Tzu

RECOGNIZE THE IMPORTANCE OF INNER PEACE:

Remember this simple and inescapable fact: You will never find lasting happiness or true success in life without inner peace.

The first step in achieving inner peace is to make it a top priority in your life. Understand and appreciate that inner peace is not an idealized state only attained by a reclusive, and monastic few. It is inherent in every human being, and well within everyone's grasp. But we all must value, claim, and protect it.

TAKE RESPONSIBILITY AND CONTROL:

You are responsible for your inner peace, and *you* are really the only one that can ensure your tranquility. Never let it depend on any one or any thing. It is much too important.

ELIMINATE NEGATIVES FIRST:

The purpose of the "Prescriptions" half of this, and every other subject, is to help you attain and maintain inner peace and beautiful living.

Always start any personal improvement program by reducing or eliminating negatives *first*.

Do not make the mistake of thinking that, if you add enough positives to your life, the negatives will diminish. They won't. Like guerrilla warriors, they just go underground and slowly erode the positives.

So start with your own *stuff*. Tackle the negatives first, head on. If you rid yourself of the things that trouble and limit you, and your inner peace will naturally arise.

TAKE YOUR CASE:

Analyze any mental afflictions you may have. This is called "case-taking." Then determine which if any of the preceding psychoanalytical schools will work best for you. Get advice in this analysis if you need it.

TRY THE COGNITIVE APPROACH:

Use Rationality:

The more rational the proceedings, the more successful will be the cognitive analysis approach to therapy. What does this mean? It means seeing, as best we can, things as they really are – the truth of reality. It also means not seeing things, as we fear they might be, or wish they were. Do not see only the negatives and not the positives of your situation.

For those who are rationalistic, the use of logic and analysis can deflate worries and reduce problems to a manageable level. A little rationality can allow us to turn the page and move on.

Realize You Are Not Alone:

Realize that others have suffered and overcome problems as great and greater than yours. You are never unique or odd in any way. Rest assured that thousands, and perhaps millions of others have experienced what ever you are grappling with. They have emerged from the darkness and you will too.

Get Perspective:

One of the healthiest ways to detoxify your mind is adopt a much more spacious view of life. Mental pathologies are often the result of an obsessionally narrowed focus. A troubled mind focuses exclusively on one person or thing. See the vast panorama of life. It is a very big world, and there are many wonderful people, places, and things in it. Find them!

Let Time Heal You:

Everything changes over time. (This is Buddhist *anicca* or impermanence). Take heart in the fact that this includes your disturbances, and wounds. They will pass too. After you remove yourself from your tormentor, no one can torture you but you.

IDENTIFY YOUR DEMONS AND DIFFICULTIES:

Prioritize:

Your inner work can be divided into two types: demons and difficulties. The demons are those more serious, deep, dark pathologies that have been there for a while. The difficulties are those more transient, garden-variety, problems of everyday living. You may not have any demons. Or you may have them, and not know it. Identify both.

DEMONS:

Take the following steps to ferret out your demons:

Sequester Yourself:

Step out of the rat race. Take some time off from your daily routine. Seclude yourself. Find a quiet place where you will not be interrupted. Meditate to settle your mind. Then contact your demons.

Face Your Demons:

Do you have a private torture chamber in the dungeons of your mind? Are there demons there that can arise at a moments notice and destroy your inner peace? If so, courageously face them.

They exist for a reason, and they have been trying to get your attention. Ask them what they want. Then listen with openness and understanding. They may exist because of a past wound; an obsession with someone or something; a health problem; a financial risk; or because of a painful relationship. Discover the nature of your demons. They are there because of some type of negative experience that is unresolved.

Now you have a choice: Let your demons continue to threaten you, or work with them until they are tame.

Believe that *every* negative experience in your life – no matter what - has potential for positive personal growth embedded in it.

Maintain an unshakable faith in the power of adversity to transform your life for the better. Find the benefit in every negative experience in your life – past, present, or future. Turn each setback or tragedy into an opportunity for your development.

CALL FOR AN ARMISTICE:

Call for a truce with your demons. Negotiate with them in good faith. Seek a win-win solution. Become partners with them and work toward a successful resolution. Win their trust. This could mean one or more of the following: analyze the hurt, fear, reactivity, or anger; understand the reason for it; develop an effective resolution such as one of the following: (reframing it, neutralizing it; detaching from it; moving on from it.) Correctly managed, your demons will never disturb you again.

What a novel idea for achieving inner peace: Don't fight with yourself.

DIFFICULTIES:

Identify Them:

After your demons are tame, begin working on your difficulties – those every day more transient problems. Look within. Uncover any concerns or disturbances that you may be harboring. Be honest with yourself. Identify and analyze them. Determine if they are real or imagined; serious or trivial; imminent or distant.

Studies on what people worry about find that a low percentage are real and actionable. In other words, most of our worries will never happen, or if they do, are trivial. There is little we can do about the rest (such as aging).

Take Action:

Directly address those concerns and problems that are relevant, and that you can do something about. Use intelligent personal management. Prioritize them.

Gather information that is relevant to a solution. Almost always, others have faced the same problem. Learn their success stories. Now develop a plan that will solve the issue or at least make it tolerable. Visualize what you would ideally like to achieve. Then be creative about developing options that will make that vision a reality.

Any plan has three basic dimensions: time, benefit, and cost. Develop the time/benefit/cost ratios for your options and then select the most desirable. And have a Plan B in your back pocket in case Plan A doesn't work.

Now implement the plan. Hell is paved with good intentions, and the universe rewards action. You must act. Methodically work on removing or greatly reducing all those difficulties in your life that diminish your inner peace.

Forget the Rest:

As for the rest of your worrisome thoughts, just forget them. Life is too short to consume one brain cell worrying about what is inconsequential or non-actionable. Turn the page. Move on.

BUILD WITH POSITIVES:

Remember who you are – a human being with astounding inherent potentials. Keep the faith in yourself. Stay centered. Be realistically optimistic. Develop an inner calm and outer simplicity. Maintain a broad perspective so that you do not get caught in trivialities. Separate the big from the little. Develop great *"te"*, or character. Tap into your natural creativity. Be dynamic. Be the person you would most like to be.

REMEMBER ACCEPTANCE:

To develop inner peace, acceptance is essential. When you think about it, most of what happens in our life is almost entirely out of our control (heredity, environment, the behavior of others.)

Set your ego aside and see that you are a part of something much greater. Recognize that we are all subject to the Tao – the eternal laws, principles, and forces of nature. Tune into, and cooperate with, this universal intelligence.

Refrain from trying to force yourself and others in an inappropriate, unnatural direction *(wu-wei)*. You will only find frustration and disaster there. Universal laws do not conform to individual preferences. Get to know them. Make peace with them. You will find a harmony, contentment, and success unattainable in any other way.

(From the West: *"For peace of mind, resign as general manager of the universe."* - Larry Eisenberg)

OUTER PEACE

DESCRIPTIONS:

INNER FIRST:

For Taoists, peace in the outside world naturally evolves from peace in the inner world. If the mind is still, and the heart is pure, there is less chance of outer conflicts.

DISENGAGEMENT VS. ENGAGEMENT:

A sure way to ensure peace with the outer world is to disengage from it. Some Taoists, including the great sage Lao Tzu, simply removed themselves from society. Other Taoists semi-isolate themselves. They live on the fringe of populations, mingling with people only for brief periods. Still others are fully engaged. They are in the "belly of the beast." For this group, the challenge to maintain outer peace is much greater.

TAOIST CONCEPTS FOR OUTER PEACE:

Introduction:

What follows is a brief description of ten topics that contribute to outer peace:

Awareness:

Being aware of the needs, wants, virtues, problems, and dispositions of others allows Taoists to better respond to them. Example: Sensitivity to a person who has experienced abuse prevents over-reaction to their abuse-related behavior.

Non-Duality:

By not making sharp distinctions, Taoists avoid divisive polarization. They know labels are artificial, and many boundaries are imaginary. Example: They avoid the endless and often violent conflicts generated by religious duality – the relentless "*My God is better than your God*" arguments.

Detachment:

Taoist detachment means that they do not let the provocative vicissitudes of the outer world - both joyous and tragic – upset their mental placidity. Hence they do not "act out." It is like having a firewall against irrationality; a governor on emotions; a flame retardant for the heart. Detaching from the outcome of personal relationships allows them to be healthier, and prevents becoming trapped in intolerable servitude. Detaching from the outcome of business ventures allows more honesty.

Enlightenment:

Enlightened Taoists automatically move away from conflict and toward harmony in their outer world as they follow the Tao. Enlightenment, among many other things, means greater perspective. This allows them to separate the important from the unimportant, and avoid petty disputes. Perspective is all. To be enlightened is to see the big picture as it truly is.

Truth:

Holding dear to the virtue of truth, Taoists avoid the inevitable problems that arise from deceit, deception, and dishonesty of any type. Truth also minimizes misunderstandings that lead to conflict and hurt.

Personal Responsibility:

Personal responsibility means there is no one to blame. No one to blame means there is no finger pointing, guilt throwing, or animosity when things do not go well. Taoists take charge of their life.

Wu-Wei:

By not forcing, Taoists avoid the reflexive animosity that inevitably arises when anyone is coerced. Living according to *wu-wui* eliminates "push-back" and passive aggressiveness in both personal and business relationships.

By not forcing, Taoists are not in a war with nature. They don't "fight" the elements, and "tame" their natural surrondings. They are aware that their outer peace would be destroyed if they pick a fight with any aspect of the natural world.

Adaptability:

The Tao is in constant flux. To maintain harmony with it, Taoists continuously adapt to changing conditions. Continuous adjustments to maintain alignment with the natural world means reduced friction in the outside world.

Feng Shui:

The art and science of *Feng Shui* encourages harmony with nature in the placement of man-made objects and structures. This allows the free flow of *chi*, which contributes to outer peace.

Wholeness:

Wholeness means inclusion. Inclusion means nothing essential is left out. Nothing essential left out means there are no missing elements to weaken operation of things.

PRESCRIPTIONS:

ALWAYS MAINTAIN CONTROL:

Do not become frustrated or angry with anyone who might be deliberately provoking you. Turn down the heat before reaching mental combustion. Keep your composure no matter how difficult others may become.
One of the best ways of doing this is to have a calm and dignified self-image. You will be less likely to be someone else.

REMEMBER THREE GENERAL OPTIONS:

If anyone is challenging your mental placidity, remember that the following three options are available to you:

1. *Suffer*:

Never suffer for very long with any one who is a threat to your inner peace. This includes a parent, "friend", lover, spouse, child, or boss. Never be an enabler, doormat, or victim for *anyone*. This does not mean that you must reject someone who might have temporarily acted out of character. There is a place for patient understanding, tolerance, and forgiveness. But there is a limit to these fine qualities as well. Do not give people a compassion that cripples. You can do too much for people and weaken them. Do not make the mistake of neglecting your responsibilities to protect and preserve yourself and your assets. Never tolerate toxic or malevolent people who drain your life energy and destroy your sacred peace.

2. Improve the situation:

Try to communicate, negotiate, or take action that fixes or at least improves the situation with the other person. Sometimes this means that you have to look at things differently. Other times it takes a good-faith mutual effort. When this is feasible, some marvelous long-term results can be achieved.

3. Leave:

When you are unable to find a way to improve your relationship with someone, then end the relationship. Never resign yourself to a life of suffering. Have the honesty to recognize the futility of the situation, and the courage and strength to change it. Don't make excuses. It may be challenging to separate yourself from others at times, but it is your right and obligation to safeguard your inner peace. Now avoiding the obvious damaging people and predatory jackals is easy. But it is very difficult when you become attached to someone and they have qualities you love and other traits that conflict. Muster all your strength, move away, and don't look back.

Independency:

Do not expect others to think, speak, act, or be as you wish. When someone is disturbing, realize that they are simply being who they are at this point on their path of personal evolution. Do not expect them to be farther along than they are. They are dealing with their own set of hereditary limitations, childhood abuses, personal mistakes, painful pathologies, and adverse conditions.

TRY *NOT* WINNING:

If you have a confrontational personality, or just some sharp edges, start today to change from pugnacity to peace. Give up the need to always be "right" and to always "win." Big people do not engage in arguments and fights. They do not let anyone draw them into combat. If someone is offensive to you, then simply distance yourself from him or her, either temporarily or permanently.

Become one with the Tao, and change from competition and combat to cooperation and compassion. Never engage in energy-draining, life-wasting disputes. Simply be above them.

DEFUSE EXPLOSIVE SITUATIONS:

Introduction:

When you are in a social or business situation that is becoming tense, take the initiative to relieve the tension and relax the combatants. There are several good ways of doing this. Change the tone from negative to positive. Sometimes one comment that conveys humility, humor, or friendliness of any kind can instantly move a relationship onto a cordial path. Here are seven ways to defuse and explosive situation with one person or a group:

Red Alert:

Call the disputant's attention to the fact that the discussion is getting emotional and irrational. This alone may calm things down. No one likes to be, or appear to be, out of control. Most of the time you will see them settle down, and take on the appearance of a mature, reasonable person.

Convey Respect:

Often arguments are the result of someone feeling like they are not respected. Make a statement that conveys your respect for others intelligence, knowledge, integrity, professionalism, feelings, and even possessions.

Remind:

Remind everyone that you are seeking a win-win solution, not a win-loose victory. Each party must be better off with the solution, or no deal.

Ask:

Ask this simple question of your antagonist: "*What are you trying to accomplish?*" Then just listen.

Humor:

It is amazing how a quip at the right moment can totally change the tone of a meeting from one of hostility to one of collegiality.

Love:

Whenever you are in a tense situation with a child, spouse, lover, relative, or friend, communicate your love for them. But before you do, try to discover how the other party wants to receive it. Some people want to hear you say it. Others want to be touched. Still others want a practical sign of it.

Time Out:

This technique works for adults as well as children. It can be done in two levels: First, just separate the two and cease hostilities for a while. Second, take time out together for something very pleasant: a drink, good meal, entertainment, or even walk in the woods. It is amazing what a change in physiology or scenery can do for the dispositions of people. Notice how friendly people are at dinner gatherings.

AWARENESS

"He who knows others is learned; He who knows himself is wise." – Lao Tzu

DESCRIPTIONS:

INTRODUCTION:

To follow the Tao, we must be aware of the Tao. Since the Tao is ever present, we must be ever aware.

Taoists excel in awareness. In this subject, we will explore the different ways Taoists are attentive. The sister concept to this one in Buddhism is called *sati*.

AWARENESS INSIDE:

Mental:

Taoists begin their awareness within. The starting point is always the mind and the thoughts it generates all day long. They are aware of their state of mind and alert to negative thought patterns. They know what a strong connection there is between their mental and emotional worlds, and control the former to ensure peace in the latter (next section). They focus on what is natural, healthy, and right for their life. There is no place for negativity or destructive thought. Just as when the sense organs are healthy clear they can sense better, so too can the mind think better when it is also is healthy and clear.

Physical:

Taoists are receptive to inner signals from their body. They monitor their physical condition, and detect when things are amiss. They are their own first responders. They know how dangerous it is to ignore or trivialize these messages. They view pain as a friendly messenger, not an enemy. Taoists do not kill (palliate) the carrier of unpleasant news with drugs or diversions. They know that the suppression of symptoms is not a cure. They listen, learn, and respond appropriately. Taoists stimulate the "vital force" within to correct the constitutional cause of any sickness. They are actively engaged in their health. Taoists harmonize with their natural inner rhythms, and monitor the progress of their holistic human development. They never make pathology a part of their social fabric.

Emotional:

Taoists stay aware of their emotional status. Inner peace is essential. That which disrupts this must be settled or avoided. Long suffering is not the way of the Tao. They note how people and things affect their attitudes, health, energy, moods, and rhythms of life.

AWARENESS OUTSIDE:

Human Environment:

Taoists are tuned to the human and man-made aspects of their outer world. They are never caught socially flat-footed. This social intelligence is important to decide who and what to include, but more importantly, what to *exclude*. Avoidance rather than inter-dependence is appropriate at times. Knowing what fits and does not fit is critical. Hell is over-sharing with those energy-drainers who are vexations to the spirit. Taoists are constantly alert to digressions, deceptions, and dangers. They intuitively know what is helpful and harmful and select accordingly. They continuously sense the social texture of their surroundings.

Natural Environment:

The goal of all Taoists is to be at one with nature. They observe the flow, patterns, and cycles of the natural world, and the dynamic interplay between themselves and their natural environment.

Taoists are realists. They do not expect the natural world to favor them. It is what it is. The universe has a constant impartiality. The sun shines on all. And earthquakes affect everyone. Nature is an equal opportunity benefactor and killer. Bad things can and do happen to the saints as well as the sinners in our world. They recognize and accept this. There is no room for self-pity.

Taoists understand that life is not always "fair." And justice is often a long time coming, if ever in this lifetime. In the short run, the unethical, immoral, and criminal sometimes seem to get away with their evil deeds. But in the long run, the inexorable laws of man and nature exact a toll on them.

(From the West: *"It is only with the heart that one can see rightly; what is essential is invisible to the eye."* – Antoine de Saint-Exupery)

PRESCRIPTIONS:

"Colors blind the eye. Sounds deafen the ear. Flavors numb the taste. Thoughts weaken the mind. Desires wither the heart. The Master observes the world but trusts his inner vision. He allows things to come and go. His heart is open as the sky." - Chapter 12 of the *Tao Te Ching*

BEGIN WITHIN (again and always):

In General:

Ceteris paribus (other things being equal), your first priority should always be attention to your current condition. Everything else in your world is dependent upon it. If you are not in good working order, it will be difficult for you to progress or to be of any help to others.

Never remain oblivious to the impact you have on others. Never ignore or trivialize transmissions from your inner world. This is especially true for any negative feedback from your body.

Regularly pause to look inward. Train yourself to be aware of your state of mind, body, and feelings. Take periodic mini-audits of your state of being. This means listening to your inner voice, physical sensations, and emotional-spiritual condition.

Your Mind:

Monitor and analyze your attention, intentions, interests, goals, motives, and overall state of mind. Ask if you are currently in an empowered or enfeebled state. When you discover that your mind is derailed, take immediate action to put it back on the right track. Without over or under reacting, make the adjustments that will restore your proper state of mind, and overall balance.

Your Body:

Pay attention to and analyze the messages your body sends you. Consider discomfort or pain to be valuable feedback from down under. Be sensitive to it, and respond promptly and intelligently. Find out what is causing your physical distresses, and seek medical help if necessary. Make sure you have regular physical exams. Get an analysis of your blood chemistry.

Your Feelings and Spiritual Well-Being:

How is your mood, and general feelings about life? Amid all your *achieving*, do not forget *being*. Being happy should be a high priority. Check your path to ensure that it is fulfilling and includes times of true joy. Make sure that your direction will take you to where you really want to go. Make sure you are self-actualizing, and applying your natural talents.

BE ALERT:

Develop an awareness of your social, structural, and natural surroundings. Be alert to covert and overt threats. They can be as subtle, and include carcinogenic food, immune-compromising stress, toxic people, and dangerous neighborhoods.

Be aware of the patterns in nature. Learn the timing of cycles. Do not attempt to force things at the wrong time. Cooperate with nature. There are seasons – in a year and in a life - to sew, to grow, to reap, and to rest. Become skilled at flowing easily with the cycles of nature. Tune in to the rhythms of life. Seek oneness with the Tao.

REMEMBER PURPOSE:

As you increase your inner and outer awareness, remember that breath of perception is important, but it must be allied with breath of purpose before either is fully effective.

(From the West: *"Thinking is more interesting than knowing, but less interesting than looking."* - Goethe)

NON-DUALITY

DESCRIPTIONS:

"*When the wise man grasps the pivot, he is in the center of the circle, and there he stands while 'Yes' and 'No' pursue each other around the circumference.*" – Chuang Tzu

INTRODUCTION:

To examine the Taoist idea of non-duality, let's first review its opposite – dualistic thinking. Then we will review non-dualistic thinking. We will then reconcile the two.

DUALISTIC THINKING:

Dualistic thinking has a proclivity toward binary thought. It divides everything into sharp polarities and labels things.

Here are some common examples of the distinctions created by dualistic thinking: up-down, left-right, light-dark, hot-cold, subject-object, us-them, mind-body, matter-energy, win-lose, right-wrong, good-evil, and all-nothing.

This divisive tendency arises in part from the left-brain hemisphere. The thinking in this half is linear, logical, sequential, and word-based. It analyzes, divides, and classifies things.

ARGUMENT SUPPORTING DUALISTIC THINKING:

Aristotle began the science of classification. Sir Isaac Newton, widely considered the greatest scientific mind of all time, invented the calculus. An aspect of it, the derivative, divides things into infinitesimally small areas. The integral then sums them according to a formula. Errors of approximation become insignificant. By dividing the area under a curve into extremely small rectangles, and then adding the individual areas of these rectangles, one can closely calculate the area under that curve.

The point here is that without division and symbolization we would not have science, as we know it.

ARGUMENTS AGAINST DUALISTIC THINKING:

Introduction:

There are three arguments against dualistic thinking:

- Confusing thoughts of reality with reality
- Forgetting relativity
- Obscuring connectivity

Confusing Thoughts Of Reality With Reality:

In Taoist thinking, the tendency to bifurcate everything into two extremes evolves from the mistaken view that these polarities have an independent self-existence. By constantly distinguishing and dividing people and things into separate parts, we fool ourselves into thinking that our artificial classifications are real. Our words and labels take on a life of their own. We become so caught up in our speech that soon we forget that we are talking about abstracts, not reality. Our artificial distinctions often narrow our perspective and therefore limit our judgment. Words are just symbols that never capture the rich complexity or reality. Hence the saying: *"The map is not the territory."* In the field of operations research, the name for this fallacy is called *hypostatization* – confusing thoughts for reality.

Forgetting Relativity:

Nature does not recognize our sharp divisions. Nature does not exist that way. Phenomena - such as light, heat, and mass - exist in a continuum, not in on/off binary states. We make our judgments and statements about a variable as though it were a constant.

Obscuring Connectivity:

Duality implies separateness, and separateness is an illusion because the Tao permeates and connects all. Dualistic thinking takes us away from this connectivity to a world apart.

NON-DUALISTIC THINKING:

Introduction:

Taoists (as well as Buddhists and Zenists) are not inclined toward dualistic thinking. They do not continuously dichotomize. They don't split everything into parts. They don't create artificial boundaries and categories. Taoists don't see absolute differences, but rather relative comparisons. Neither do they see mutually exclusive opposites.

A Chinese character captures the Taoist non-judgmental, state of mind - *wu-nien*. *Wu* means "not" and *nien* means "the heart-mind." *Wu-nien* is the clear, direct perception of realty without man-made names and structures.

ARGUMENT SUPPORTING NON-DUALITY:

Introduction:

There are three arguments supporting non-dualistic thinking that are the mirror image of the three arguments against dualistic thinking:

- It brings us closer to reality
- It is relativistic
- It supports connectivity

It brings us closer to reality:

A qualified interpretation and application of non-dualistic thinking has merit. There is a place for the clear, direct perception of realty without artificial names and structures. This wide-eyed view of the world, and "beginners mind" favors objectivity – a necessity for truth. It also opens the possibility of seeing things in a new way. This is especially important when the old ways are no longer effective. Additionally, non-dualistic thinking prepares the way to understand the Buddhist concepts of connectedness, dependence, and *shunyata* (emptiness).

It is relativistic:

Taoists believe polarities define each other.

"Under heaven all can see beauty as beauty only because there is ugliness. All can know good as good only because there is evil. Therefore having and not having arise together. Difficult and easy compliment each other. Long and short contrast each other; High and low rest upon each other; Voice and sound harmonize each other; Front and back follow one another...." – Chapter-2 of the *Tao Te Ching*

Everything is relative. Our descriptions have little relevance without a sense of scale. Opposing pairs of complimentary opposites provide this reference. Taoists see the truth of this and thereby more accurately understand reality. A good way to grasp this is to think on the grandest of scales. Consider the universe. It is infinite. There is no absolute up or down, short or long.

It supports connectivity:

Taoist non-dualistic thinking encourages the recognition of connectivity. If the Tao permeates all, then everything has a common base. Everything is connected. We are all made out of the same "stuff", and animated by the same forces. This non-reductive inclusion allows Taoists to transcend the egotistical self, and better interconnect with the totality of life.

RECONCILIATION OF DUALISM AND NON-DUALISM:

We are endowed with left-brain linear, logical, analytical, and dualistic faculties that allow us to see differences. There is a legitimate need for this mental faculty and for this process.

We are also endowed with right brain, holistic, holographic, intuitive, non-dualistic faculties that allow us to see continuums. We need this power as well.

Nature (The Tao) did not give us both ways of seeing the world so that we would have to choose one and ignore the other. We should not deny parts of ourselves that are natural. Nature does nothing in vain. Half our brain is not disposable. Both are important.

(From the West: "*Convictions are more dangerous enemies of truth than lies.*" – Nietzsche)

PRESCRIPTIONS:

"*To set up what you like against what you dislike – this is the disease of the mind.*" – *Seng-T'San*

AVOID THE BINARY TRAP:

Do not fall into the trap of believing that you have to choose one way of thinking over another. There is a place for non-judgmental, unsymbolized, objective, thinking without categorization. There is also a place for discrimination, classification, and systemization.

ADAPT YOUR THINKING:

Use non-dualistic thinking when dealing with phenomena that varies on a spectrum of values (intelligence, health, wealth, temperature, light, etc.). Learn to appreciate the interconnectedness of the world.

Use dualistic thinking when dealing with phenomena that exists in a binary condition (digital electronics, marital status, pregnancy, etc.). While "up" and "down" may be arbitrary and relative, they are useful conventions that allow us to orient our self and navigate in space.

Learn to know when to use the one, and when to use the other. It is situational. Few recommendations can be given here. But apply the template of reasonableness and practicality.

If you are researching a new phenomenon, keep a very open mind, and consider possibilities. If you are communicating to a person or group, do so in the language they understand, which include some jargon. What matters is truthful, constructive, and effective communication, not dual/non-dual thinking.

(From the West: *"A belief is not merely an idea the mind possesses; it is an idea that possesses the mind."*
– Robert Bolton)

DETACHMENT

"Have much and be confused." – Lao Tzu from the *Tao Te Ching*

DESCRIPTIONS:

INTRODUCTION:

As presented here, detachment is not emotional nihilism. It is not a lack of feeling.

Detachment is a healthy perspective and self-security that recognizes the changing nature of people and things and the futility of hanging on to them. It is an absence of insecurity, fear, obsessions, and craving.

Remember that detachment can actually improve the quality of relationships. There is a Zen saying: "*The bird of paradise does not alight on the hand that grasps.*"

WESTERN CULTURAL BACKGROUND:

Western society convincingly portrays *the good life* as one flowing from externals - especially popularity and wealth. There is an appropriate time and place for these in our journey through life. While there are many healthy examples of them, there are also many unhealthy examples. The latter often arise from the imbalance of excess by those who become mesmerized by someone or something, and lose track of what is really important. The more they listen and follow the extreme socio-economic siren calls of our culture, the more they become lost in unrestrained desire, possession, ambition, acquisition, greed, and consumption. Unhealthy attachments to others and to things lead to tacky human melodramas, and soul-eroding indulgences.

To dramatize the suffering that attachment can bring, what follows are two generic stories. They are unfortunately all too common. (The reader can reverse the genders if that would be more applicable.)

ATTACHMENT TO PEOPLE:

He meets her. Her smile brings the titillation of delightful expectations. Propelled by unfulfilled psychological and physiological needs, he projects his favorite fantasies on to her. Soon in his eyes, her persona matches his dream. His wish secretly fosters his thought. Objectivity is gone. The truth of reality is blurred by desire. A powerful delusion develops. All that he wants, she is in his eyes - despite warning signals to the contrary. He hears and sees what pleases him. And he blocks the rest. His image of her becomes everything he has longed for in a woman. She is his dream come true. Flirtation turns to romance; romance to affection; affection to love.

Her voice becomes the sweetest sound in his world. Her appearance is the light in his life. Her gentle touch is the most wonderful of sensations. Her movements are a hypnotic poetry of motion. He is drunk on desire, and lost in love. He has become hopelessly, obsessively, compulsively, under her spell. He is intoxicated with her. She is his addiction. She haunts his thoughts day and night and has become his passionate predilection. It's witchcraft.

The gentle petals of intimacy gracefully begin to open. If he crosses the Rubicon, strong bonds form at a whole new level. She becomes imprinted on his body and soul.

She has achieved a social hegemony over him. His life becomes completely skewed toward her. Soon he begins to neglect his former interests, activities, and even responsibilities. That which held his attention before is now irrelevant. He even begins to ignore his family and friends. She is all that matters. He finds himself waiting and anticipating her call. He craves any opportunity to communicate or to be with her. And he even invents clever ways to contact her.

But she is centered on herself, and aloof to others. She is a narcissistic vixen. Sensing her power, she looks to him to feed her vanity and for exploitative value. She becomes manipulative. In his great desire to keep her attention and please her, he ignores his own principles and beliefs, and joins her in every frivolity. Setting aside his pride and self-respect, he acquiesces to her every wish, obediently does her bidding, and even takes her occasional abuse. He becomes her de facto slave.

Then as surely as autumn follows summer, she becomes bored with this game of hearts and begins to lose interest in him. She begins to be emotionally distant, and physically unavailable. The distance becomes greater until there is no contact at all. This is the slow kill. Alternatively, she goes for the sudden death option. Possibly after exaggerating some real or imagined issue, she works up a head of steam and lets him have it. In a cold, calculating way, she fillets him like a tuna.

At first, he is in denial. Surely something so "perfect" could not go so wrong. He begins to compromise himself even more for her. Desperation and even panic sets in. He neurotically imagines every sort of painful, self-deprecating possibility. With each one, he drives a stake into his own heart. The pain and sorrow is unbearable. He has grown as *attached* to her as a Siamese twin. And the separation is as painful as a surgery without anesthesia.

He no longer sleeps or eats very much. He looses interest in life. He begins to neglect himself and his duties. He is no longer rational, healthy, stable, or productive. His family and friends no longer recognize him. He is a trivial effigy of his once happy and animated self. Destroyed by the loss of her, he walks around like the living dead. Life has no meaning. In his despair and depression, he begins to abuse alcohol and drugs. He has lost his way, his job, his friends, and his soul. And what was his essential mistake at the core of his demise? *Attachment.*

One of the saddest scenarios in the above depiction involves what is sometimes called *crazy making*. That is when a parent, friend, spouse, or significant other is good to you at one time, and hurts you another. And this sick cycle continues until the victim either tears away or is psychologically destroyed. *Crazy making* is often perpetrated by a split personality. Unfortunately, the victim sometimes becomes one as well, especially when they are a child who is struggling to understand and develop social responses.

ATTACHMENT TO POSITION AND POSSESSIONS:

Once again the following depiction applies equally to both genders.

Our next subject is attached to money and possessions. He is greedy. As a younger man, he ignores the good advice to enter a career that he loves and uses his natural talents. Instead of developing his own definition of *success*, he is seduced by opportunism. Ignoring his innate potentials, true calling, and passionate interests, he eagerly enters the fast track to the American Dream. Despite those inner messages and warning signs, he ambitiously begins to claw his way up the money ladder.

All along the way, he aggressively builds the right professional connections, masters the faker's minuet, and shamelessly panders to influential people. He insensitively exploits others; cleverly manipulates the system; ruthlessly grabs power; secretly abuses his positions of trust; callously neglects his family and friends; and heartlessly ignores the suffering of others that he creates along the way. He places personal gain above ethics, or even above plain common decency. At the top of his game, he arrogantly displays the ostentatious trappings of success, and superciliously indulges in them. He not only wants the applause of his peers, but also their *envy*. He recognizes no point of sufficiency in his ego-delights. For him there is no such thing as *enough* - regardless of the human, material, or environmental cost. There is only the obsession for more.

However, the pleasures of his indulgences fill his rapacious desires only momentarily. They have an intrinsic air of social urgency at first. But the giddiness wanes and the novelty of these superficial externals soon fade. He once again has to face his inner emptiness.

Being addicted to narcissism and consumerism, he soon needs another *fix*. His dependency drives him off in hot pursuit of yet another novelty or thrill, sometimes a costly or risky one.

All along, his fragile sense of self rises and falls with external measures of success. He hungers for recognition and applause. He lives and dies in this shallow, soul-destroying culture of individual and institutionalized delusion.

DETACHMENT:

Awareness:

Taoists know that externals – people, popularity, power, and possessions – can never satisfy our endless, insatiable, ego-driven, desires. Nor can they bring any lasting peace or happiness. On the contrary, Taoists are aware of the trap of attachment. They see that we are vulnerable to the capricious nature of people, and to the inherent emptiness of things. They view our attachment to, and dependency on, externals as the root cause of our misery. (The second Noble Truth in Buddhism). They see how covetousness, craving, and clinging leads to anxiety, tension, disappointment, self-criticism, envy, jealousy, and frustration. In a psycho-emotional sense, attachment prevents us from reaching what embryologists call the "age of viability."

Control:

Taoists believe it is easier to control the first desire than to satisfy all those that follow.

By ceasing desiring and grasping, and by ending the dependence on externals, they maintain control of their destiny. They do not allow themselves to be puppets that are continually manipulated by social and commercial interests. They avoid the innumerable traps and entanglements of the human and material world. They are slaves to no one or no thing. Their minds and hearts are their own. By liberating themselves from the endless chase, they are free to live a simple, tranquil, and authentic life.

ADVENTURES IN DETACHMENT

Two stories from the life of Chuang Tzu provide a sense of his degree of detachment:

THE STORY OF CHUANG TZU'S VISIT TO KING WEN

King Wen (Wei) of Chou (Chu) sent a messenger bearing expensive gifts to entice Chuang Tzu to join his court and assume a prestigious ministerial position. This was a great honor. While acknowledging it, he politely declined. He amusingly analogized people that assume these privileged offices as sacred animals. These unknowing pitiful creatures are decorated and fattened on the "good life", but eventually walk to their sacrificial death wishing they were uncelebrated and unknown little pigs playing in the mud.

THE STORY OF THE DEATH OF CHUANG TZU'S WIFE

At the death of his wife, Chuang Tzu was unusually composed. He had none of the usual signs of grief and loss that would be characteristic of such occasions. He was questioned about this apparent heartlessness. His response was that for him to lose his composure or grieve over her death would mean that he was ignorant of natural law, which he was not. He believed that her death was not an *end*, but rather just another phase of her continuous existence in various states as she transforms through time. She existed in many different forms before her birth, and in life. She now still exists in death, albeit in a different form. So therefore she is not lost. Hence there is no reason to grieve. (Could this perspective help us in the West?)

(From the West: "Attachment is the great fabricator of illusions; reality can be attained only by someone who is detached." – Simone Weil)

PRESCRIPTIONS:

"How shall I grasp it? Do not grasp it. That which remains when there is no more grasping is the self." - Panchadasi

RECOGNIZE IMPERMANENCE (Buddhist *Anicca*):

Recognize that the universe is in a constant state of transformation.

See that all things change. Everything that has a beginning has an ending. This includes your thoughts, suffering, relationships, possessions, and your existence on Earth. Knowing this will help you to understand why it is so irrational and hazardous to attach to anyone or anything.

> Note: I believe there is one exception to the statement that *"All things change."* And that is truth. Eternal truths never change, and they include the laws of nature (Tao) and all that has really happened. More on this under *"Ch'ang"* in the "Philosophy of Taoism - Metaphysics."

NEVER ATTACH:

Your well-being and even survival depends on you remembering to NEVER attach!

The instant you attach, you have put yourself at risk. You are no longer a master of your destiny, but a slave to it. You become vulnerable to unwanted changes in who or what you attached to. At the very least, this means you will experience the discomfort of instability of things not being as they were. But it can be much worse. Develop strong attachments, and you can become weakly dependent, insecure, worried, disappointed, sad, frustrated, angry, critical, irrational, desperate, and severely depressed.

Despite every inclination to do so, do not set your self up for suffering. Do not let those mental and emotional connections become so strong that you lose your sense of objectivity, or worse yet, your sense of self. Never hand the controls of your mind, emotions, or life over to anyone.

Detachment also applies to the material side of your life. Do not cling to money or possessions. They too pass. And always remember that you really cannot "take it with you." At the end of life, all of your material possessions become irrelevant. Maybe the box you go into is a little fancier, but the wealthiest and the poorest end up in the same place. Do not become so enamored and intrigued by anything that it takes on an inflated importance in your life.

"KNOW THYSELF":

Heed the wise statement of Socrates that was inscribed on the Greek temple at Delphi: *"Know thyself."* This is necessary to take the step that follows.

Develop an understanding of your vast, unique, and untapped potential, and what you would be if this potential were fully developed. In this process of self-discovery, exhaustively explore the powerful triumvirate of your mind, body, and emotions. This is what psychologists call *autognosis* – knowledge of self.

Be aware of your values. Make three lists - your A's, B's and C's. A's are things that are critical to you and you will never compromise. B's are things you have an opinion on, but are negotiable and might change. C's are things that you have no interest in and will relinquish to others.

Then develop a clear, inspirational, vision of what you could ultimately do and be with your best potentials. Three methods to help you discover your hidden capabilities are: introspect (meditate!), ask others, and take tests.

DEVELOP INTELLIGENT RELATIONSHIPS

Detachment does not mean disengaging from the world. That is not possible. We are all dependent to some degree in some way.

Theory is always easier than practice. Prescription is simple in the abstract and difficult in the particular. Nevertheless, be selective and progressive about your relationships with people and things. This demands the greatest of insight, wisdom, and control.

After really getting to understand yourself, find intelligent togetherness (F.I.T.) in your relationships. Do an audit on your existing relationships. Ask yourself if they are an asset or a liability. Then judge if the benefit is worth the cost. Be honest! Be careful and selective in developing new relationships. Remember that some people will take your time, use your goodwill, drain your energy, and even consume your resources. They are covertly parasitic. Others are outright toxic and dangerous.

Only be in relationships that are mutually beneficial. Both of you must be better off for the interaction. Always analyze the return on your investment of time, effort and resources from whom and what you share.

Consider those activities, people, and things holding the most promise of positive long-term return. Drop those activities, people, and things that fall below your threshold of return on personal and financial investment. Hell is over sharing. But always be sensitive and tactful in disengaging. Remember to *"Do no harm."*

The idea is to create only high-level, sweet synergies with people and things. Both you and they must benefit (win-win) with the least cost to each.

Remember that detachment can actually improve the quality of relationships. It can deepen love.

AN ADVANCED PRESCRIPTION:

All of us will face the death of a loved one at some time in our life. Study the story of the death of Chuang Tzu's wife in "Adventures in Detachment." As an advanced prescription, develop the powerful perspective of Chuang Tzu such that you will not fall apart at the death of a loved one, but rather see their death as a transformation as he did.

(From the West: *"He is richest who is content with the least, for content is the wealth of nature."* – Socrates)

HAPPINESS

DESCRIPTIONS:

"My opinion is that you never find happiness until you stop looking for it. My greatest happiness consists precisely in doing nothing whatever that is calculated to obtain happiness: and this, in the minds of most people, is the worst possible course." – Chuang Tzu

THE COMMERCIAL VIEW:

We are propagandized to believe that we need to attain certain attractive human and material conditions before we can be happy. The premise is that *when* we obtain these conditions, we will be happy. Until then, we are destined to remain empty and unfulfilled. It is as though we are somehow inherently deficient, and can only be complete by the addition of some one, or some thing.

THE TAOIST VIEW:

The Taoist view is entirely different. They believe that we limit our capacity for happiness by making it dependent upon something outside of us. By establishing commercial and other external conditions for personal satisfaction, we create costly dependencies and miss where it really is. We doom ourselves to a life of anxiety-filled struggle and frustration. We will never be truly happy when we are always looking for some one or some thing to make us happy. No one or no thing can *make you* happy. Those that believe so are always chasing a mirage and are never content.

Taoists have a far more liberated and empowered view of happiness. The logic is simple: Since the Tao is everywhere; the opportunity to be happy must also be everywhere. With faith in our inherent completeness and inner strength, we can be in good spirits anytime, anywhere, doing anything.

This includes mundane activities without any artificial, external dependencies. All we have to do is not force (*wu-wei*), be at peace, and live in harmony with the graceful flow of the Tao.

THE HEDONISTIC PARADOX:

Taoists believe that we cannot force happiness. In fact, we cannot even directly achieve it. Almost like your shadow, happiness moves away from you if you chase it, and moves toward you as you ignore it.

This is the same conclusion reached by Western philosophers in the concept of the *hedonistic paradox*. Here happiness cannot be pursued directly. It seems only to be derived indirectly from worthy activities. Chuang Tzu especially warns that the minute we establish the polarities of "happiness" and "unhappiness" and establish the former as "an object to be obtained" and the latter as "an object to avoid" we have become deluded and alienated from happiness. He is saying that by setting an objective, we are narrowing where happiness is found. Instead, his idea is to not categorize happiness, but find it in non-seeking and non-action everywhere by being at one with the Tao. So paradoxically, happiness requires not striving for happiness.

(From the West: *"It is good to have an end to journey toward; but it is the journey that matters in the end."* - Ursula K. LeGuin)

PRESCRIPTIONS:

"Feel yourself being quietly drawn by the deeper pull of what you truly love." - Rumi, the 13th century Persian-Afghan poet and philosopher

RETHINK YOUR CONCEPTS OF HAPPINESS:

If you hold a conditional view of happiness, that is if your happiness *depends* on some one or some thing outside of you, rethink the linkage. If you make a person, place or thing a condition for your happiness, you will forever be held hostage by those very conditions. Why set up these unnecessary and burdensome requirements? Why make yourself so dependent? Why put such power into someone else's hands? And that someone may or may not have your best interests at heart. In fact, they may get a sadistic delight in tormenting you. Why limit your joy to such a small piece of life? Why cheat yourself and others from countless opportunities for shared joy? Decide if you want to be a master or slave.

LET GO OF YOUR ARTIFICIAL CONDITIONS FOR HAPPINESS

Do yourself a great favor and break all of your self-imposed dependencies for happiness. Liberate yourself. Detach your idea of happiness from all externals. Look within. That's where your source of happiness has always been and always will be. If you can't find it there, you will not find it anywhere. To prove this, recall the times you were in some very pleasant place doing something enjoyable, and yet you were numb to it all. Conversely, recall the times when you were in an unpleasant situation, but inexplicably still remained peaceful or even joyful. This proves the essential primacy and power of your inner world.

CREATE AN EMPOWERING CONCEPT OF HAPPINESS:

Create a new concept of happiness that is unconditional - without temporal or spatial restrictions. Expand the time and territorial range for your joyfulness to include the totality of your life. View happiness as a natural by-product of living authentically, naturally, spontaneously, and fully in the moment. Develop a positive expectancy about your future. Feel liberated and empowered because your happiness is self-generated.

DO WHAT YOU ENJOY:

You may be tempted to be opportunistic, and work at something that is distasteful to you strictly for the egoistic or monetary gain. If so, remember these words from Lao Tzu:

"*In work, do what you enjoy.*" - Chapter 8 of the *Tao Te Ching*

What a common sense idea: Do what you enjoy. Of course do so within the bounds of decency and legality.

(From the West: "*Happiness is not a destination; it's a way of traveling.*" – Unknown)

ENLIGHTENMENT

"*Can you coax your mind from its wandering and keep to the original oneness? Can you let your body become supple as a newborn child's? Can you cleanse your inner vision until you see nothing but the light?*" - Chapter 10 of the *Tao Te Ching*

DESCRIPTIONS:

HARMONY:

In the philosophy of Taoism, to be <u>enlightened</u> is to be completely at one with the Tao. This is the highest aim of Taoist meditation. (See next subject.)

Being enlightened means returning (See "*Fu*" under "Metaphysics") to one's original, pure, elemental state (See "*Pu*" under "Ethics"). The mind is calm, and the soul is at peace. There is an undisturbed constancy. Enlightenment in Taoism is termed *ming* or "luminosity."

WU-WEI:

Non-doing or *wu-wei* (See "*Wu-Wei*" under "Ethics") is a fundamental Taoist concept. Where enlightenment exists, no supplemental action is necessary because things are moving exactly in accordance with their fundamental natures. Things are as they should be, so what is there to "manage"? To be striving and doing would imply a discordant condition inconsistent with the spiritual perfection of enlightenment. Where nothing is left to be done, nothing should be done.

HSIN:

Enlightenment is not a cold, cerebral place. It is infused with *hsin*. The Chinese word *hsin* translates as "heart-mind." The enlightened realm of being is only attained when the mind tunes into the great wisdom of the heart.

"GOOD" AND "BAD" FORTUNE:

Introduction:

If the Tao includes all, how do we interpret "good" and "bad" fortune? When personal, financial, social, and natural disasters befall us, how do we keep from becoming depressed, angry, bitter, and resentful?

An important part of Taoist enlightenment is seeing the true nature of "good" and "bad" fortune. Here are three parts of this understanding:

Causation:

First, everything that eventuates – "good" and "bad" - does so because of antecedent causes and conditions. In other words, everything happens for a reason. There is no irrationality; we often just do not understand the underlying dynamics of the laws of the

Tao. Taoists understand the true nature of their misfortune, and therefore it weighs less on them.

Attachment:

Second, the enlightened mind knows that when we begin to feel like we are on an emotional roller coaster. This is a sure sign that we becoming too attached to someone or something. It is time to back away, regain our senses, and reaffirm our direction along our sacred path.

Impermanence:

Third, the enlightened mind is aware that all people and things continuously flow and change. Situations do as well. Good or bad today might turn out to be its opposite in a day, week, month, or year. Often the greatest tragedies, especially those that seem to have no redeeming value, eventually become the catalysts that bring us the most positive transformations we ever experience.

PRESCRIPTIONS:

VISUALIZE:

Let enlightenment be your guiding principle. Visualize your original nature as enlightened – free of disturbing thoughts and feelings, residing in the constant composure of *wu-wei* non-action, and above all, in harmony with the Tao. Meditate on enlightenment. See and feel yourself in this magnificent state.

STAY ON COURSE:

Avoid any thoughts, words, or actions that might take you away from this sublime state. When you stray from the Tao, take action to return.

IN TIMES OF TROUBLE:

Remember Causation:

Whenever fate seems to be working against you, remember that there is a rational reason, a cause and effect in play. The event or situation did not just "happen", it developed from prior actions and conditions. If you examine the past carefully, you will most likely find that you played a part as well. Perhaps you were simply in the wrong place at the wrong time, but you did choose to be there. Realize that there really isn't any "good" or "bad" luck, it is all cause and effect. The universe is not pro or con. It flows with the Tao with a cool indifference.

Remember Detachment:

Ask yourself what your relationship is to the person or event that caused you to feel that you experienced bad luck. Ask yourself if you lost your objectivity, became connected, and started to grasp. Maybe all this was the result of a false assumption. For instance, that someone would always be there for you, or that they would always tell you the truth. The reasons for self-deception are many. Remember that no one and no thing are with us forever. Everything that has a beginning has an ending. No one promised us that they would be with us forever. No one promised us that they were perfect and would never lie or deceive us.

Remember Impermanence:

When events seem to move against you, remember that everything (except truth) changes. Eventually you may find that the event is much less deleterious than you initially thought. You may learn, as so many have, that your worst nightmare turns into a catalyst for your most important developmental transformation.

Even if neither of these occurs, you will find that events will change again, this time in your favor. Remember that everything cycles. If you stay aligned with the Tao and live authentically, sooner or later you will gain or regain inner peace and beautiful living.

(From the West: *"The telling thing about a person's life is their relationship to the infinite."* – Dr. Carl Jung)

MEDITATION

DESCRIPTIONS:

WHAT MEDITATION IS NOT:

Relax. To practice and benefit from meditation, it is not necessary to convert to any ancient mystical tradition. Nor is it necessary to dress in robes, chant, burn incense, light candles, or for that matter do anything truly foreign to your lifestyle. Meditation is not a mysterious religious ritual practiced by a mystical few who uncomfortably sit in the lotus position for hours while navel-gazing. Nor is it being in a trancelike state while magical *mantra* chanting.

Contrary to what many people believe, meditation is also not a state of vacuous thoughtlessness. It is not cognitive nihilism. To eliminate all thought from the mind for prolonged periods could weaken an important mental function – our ability to conceptualize. Besides, no thought at all on a conscious or subconscious level would mean that we were brain dead.

WHAT MEDITATION IS:

Meditation is sustained mental concentration.

The object of concentration depends on the purpose of the meditation. The object can take many forms including: a feeling (the breath, the heartbeat, love, compassion), a sound (mantra), or an object (candle, stature, or symbol of a virtue) or even (as the Zenists are fond of saying) "our everyday life."

BRAIN STATES:

Brain researches have identified the following five levels of mental activity with approximate brain wave frequencies:

1. Beta (Awake): 14 cycles per second
2. Alpha: 13-8 cycles per second
3. Theta: 7-5 cycles per second
4. Delta: 1-4 cycles per second
5. REM: Rapid Eye Movement

During our sleep, we cycle through these stages at approximate 90-minute intervals.

THE ALPHA STATE:

Meditation, music, or even self-hypnosis can bring our mind into the alpha state. There, the critical thinking of the left hemisphere is subdued, and we become more receptive and retentive of information.

So the alpha state facilitates learning, and programming our mind for self-development. We can use self-talk or even taped affirmations to conduct what modern psychologists call *heterogenic conditioning*. This is a very powerful way to transform our mind and life for peace and success.

Affirmations form the connective tissue between aspiring and being.

DO ANIMALS MEDITATE?

Many believe that animals meditate. And they seem to do it naturally without instructions. Observe the stillness and seeming quiet minds of dogs, cats, birds, and countless other animals. What are they not thinking? Do they know something we don't?

PARADOXES:

Meditation embodies seemingly paradoxical opposites. It is a procedurally simple, yet personally challenging. When it seems most difficult, you need it the most. It eases the mind, yet heightens awareness. It has immeasurable benefits, yet no measurable cost.

MEDITATION IN THE EAST:

It is hard to find a spiritual path in the East that does *not* recognize the benefits of meditation (*dhyana*). Millions of people in the East have practiced meditation for thousands of years. Meditation plays a prominent role in Taoism, Buddhism and Zenism. Though there are similarities, all three traditions have a slightly different style and emphasis in the practice.

TWO BASIC TYPES OF MEDITATION:

There are many forms of meditation but they are often grouped into two general types: *samatha* and *vipassana.*

<u>*Samatha* Meditation:</u>

We are constantly distracted by random thoughts. We are also diverted by sensory overload from the cacophony of the modern world. The aim in *samatha* meditation is to simply calm the mind and bring it back to a sustained, single-pointed mental focus. Without forcing thoughts out of the mind, this practice just recognizes the various transitional states of mind and lets them pass on. As the meditation continues, the subject reaches deeper levels of awareness called the *dhyanas*.

<u>*Vipassana* Meditation:</u>

This practice picks up where *samatha* meditation leaves off. Once the mind is under control, *vipassana* or insight meditation begins the search for deeper truths of existence. It is called *insight meditation* because it leads to deep insights about the true nature and character of the self and reality. Points of focus include compassion, *metta* (loving kindness), *anicca* (impermanence), *shunyata* (emptiness), *anatta* (no-self), the *skandhas* (five elements of the self), and even death and dying. It is advisable to practice *vipassana* meditation with the support of a personal instructor who can judge the needs of the meditator and adjust the point of focus accordingly.

TAOIST MEDITATION:

Many consider meditation to be the core of Taoism. It is sometimes called "entering stillness." Taoists have a holistic view of meditation, and use it to unify and balance the mind, body, spirit, and especially the flow of *chi*. They look deep within and gently uncover buried problems, pain and sickness. By ending denial, and recognizing sensitive issues, they are able to resolve them or better coexist with them. Taoist meditation progresses by purifying the mind, body, and emotions and eventually attaining a state free from all motivated action.

Advanced Taoist mediators can direct *chi* along the

body's meridians (electric circuits) to various muscles and organs to enhance strength and health, and thereby build their *pneuma* or vital life force. They also meditate to free stagnant *chi* – the origin of aches, pains, and even diseases such as cancer.

Taoist meditation differs from other traditions in that Taoists practice meditation not only in the sitting position, but also lying, standing, and even walking. The idea is to integrate meditation into daily life as much as possible. In one practice called *Hosing-ch'i*, the meditator lies flat on the floor and visualizes the breath circulating through all parts of the body. There are many forms of Taoist meditative breathing techniques.

Like all other aspects of Taoist life, meditative practice must be in accord with nature. With respect to *wu-wei*, nothing is forced and the session is never over done. In *To Wang* – the highest level of absorption - meditators do not focus on either an inner or outer object, but simply let the mind hover unfettered to achieve oneness with the Tao.

MEDITATION IN THE WEST:

Pop Culture:

Aside from a minority of Asian mystics, serious students, and experimental bohemians in the West, meditation was relatively unknown in the West until it became popular during the counterculture movement of the 1960's. *Transcendental meditation* classes sprang up everywhere, and healers began to add it to their repertoire. Although interest waned as pop culture moved on to the next novelty, meditation gained a foothold in the West. Asian masters and Americans educated by them began to teach classes and even establish meditation centers in major American cities. Slowly, a solid base of practitioners began to develop.

From Anomaly To Alternative To Acceptance:

Despite growing evidence that meditation was a natural, non-invasive, effective therapeutic modality, powerful American medical-pharmaceutical interests steadfastly dismissed it as an anomaly. After all, it had three major strikes against it: It was not invented here (the "N.I.H. factor"). It was not high-tech. And, most damningly, it could not be patented and sold with a 500% profit margin.

It was not until the 1990's that mainstream American medicine began to recognize meditation and other highly efficacious natural healing approaches including acupuncture and herbal remedies. (Though they had proven their efficacy for thousands of years in the East.) In response to public pressure, the Western medical establishment reluctantly began to consider these methods, but marginalized them under the label *alternative medicine*. However, the term "alternative" tacitly implied "in place of." This created the risk that the consumer of health services might realize that they now had a better option to invasive, painful, often ineffective, and always expensive interventions.

The public was slowly learning that the "miracle drugs" they were addicted to may be unnecessary, and even damaging. Worse, the radiation and chemotherapy "attack and conquer" approach to treat cancer not only often failed, but it compromised the very systems and "vital force" necessary to heal the patient.

By 1987, over half of Americans favored complete legalization of alternatives. In 1991, the *U.S. Office of Alternative Medicine* was founded within the *National Institute of Health*. By 1997, 42% of Americans were using alternative medicine. Tellingly, they were paying out of pocket for over half of it. In 1999, the prestigious *Memorial Sloan-Kettering Hospital* opened an *Integrated Medical Center*.

These were disturbing developments to some of the powerful medical monopolists who controlled the nearly trillion dollar medical economy. So meditation and other natural healing methods were tucked under the huggy banner of *integrative medicine* where it could be closely watched and controlled.

Meditation – a common practice in the East for at least three thousand years – was finally semi-legitimized in the West late in the 20th century.

More people could benefit from meditation if they were "open-minded" to it. Meditation is our birthright, a natural and free process for all human beings, and perhaps animals as well. Can you think of any activity that brings such comfort for so little cost?

SEVEN WAYS TO BENEFIT FROM MEDITATION:

Introduction:

In this section, we will explore some of the many ways meditation can heal and transform you. I have grouped them under the below seven headings. An explanation of each follows.

1. Taming the *Monkey Mind*
2. Healing the Body
3. Discovering the Self
4. Creating a Buffer Zone
5. Increasing Awareness
6. Finding Answers
7. Transforming

Reminder:

Our task here is to become free of all unhealthy entanglements, and to find inner peace and beautiful living.

BENEFIT-1: TAMING THE *MONKEY MIND:*

<u>Remove Negatives First:</u>

When you want to improve *any* area of your life, remember this simple rule: All other things being equal, eliminate negatives before seeking positives.

We wouldn't hike with rocks in our pockets, or swim with weights in our suit. Why live with disturbing thoughts? When we have "something on our mind" it drains our mental, physical, and emotional resources. It is like trying to run a program on your computer while a virus in the background consumes CPU power. The first and most fundamental use of meditation is to rid our mind of viruses; to stop the chatter; and to achieve a baseline of stillness.

<u>The Monkey Mind:</u>

The mind is the monkey's playground. During our waking hours, we carry on an inner monolog of discursive talk. Our attention continually swings from one branch of thought to another every few seconds. Meditation instructors often refer to this cognitive chaos as our *monkey mind.*

The monkey swings to old branches of thought attached to a panoply of emotions from happiness and reverie, to regret and pain. Then he swings to new branches of thought attached to emotions from excitement and anticipation, to anxiety and fear.

The *monkey mind* can cause three types of problems, which I refer to as the "3-D's": digression, distortion, and destruction.

<u>Digression:</u>

Like a self-centered child, the monkey hijacks our

plans, sidetracks our attention, and narrows our perception to his every whim. Recall the times when you "lost" a slice of your life because you were preoccupied with a thought. Here are three examples:

- Needing to reread a paragraph (possibly this one) because the monkey was occupying your attention

- Asking someone to repeat what he or she said because you were chasing the monkey somewhere

- Driving a distance without remembering where you were because the monkey took over your mental steering wheel

Usually the problems of preoccupation with the monkey are minor, but they can be serious. There have been countless automobile and industrial accidents resulting in injuries and death because of the digressive monkey.

Distortion:

The monkey is a spin-doctor par excellence. He can distort reality with preconceptions, misrepresentations, and expectations. (He is certainly not a Zenist.) Listening to the diatribe of this skillful minister of propaganda can corrupt our objectivity and judgment.

Destruction:

Every once in a while, our monkey mind swings in a very dark direction, and visits a swamp of mental monsters. If not brought immediately back to a safe path, the reptiles of thought can eat us alive. They inflict every type of cognitive corruption including depression, greed, desire, anxiety, fear, anger, hostility, rage, addictions, and severe pathologies. Left uncontrolled, the dark psycho monkey can cause us spasms of panic and eventually destroy our mind, body, emotions, and life.

Commit to Meditating:

If we are ever to tame the "3-D's" of our insidious monkey, we should practice meditation on a regular basis. Meditation tames the monkey. It brings a peaceful self-censorship to our life. Beginners can spend as little as 10 to 15 minutes a day.

The quality of the meditative session is more important than the duration. And the dedication to regular meditation is most important of all.

Letting Thoughts Go:

The idea here is not to stop thoughts, but to let them stop by themselves, especially those that cause the Chinese water torture of pain. Just let them arise like a soap bubble, float along for a brief moment on the pond of your conscious, and then watch them dissolve. Don't grasp them or add to them. Put your mind in a passive fetal position.

Object of Attention in Meditation:

To tame the monkey, the object of attention can be something very simple like the breath or a candle. Exclusive focus on an object calms the mind, body, and emotions. Bringing ones attention to the breath helps to eliminate disturbing thoughts. Properly done, it is instantly relaxing. Continue this single-pointed focus. Cease your inner chatter. Calm your emotions. Decompress the tension. Regain perspective. End the madness of war with the monkey on the battlefield of your mind.

Non-Thinking:

Meditation is like a mental mouthwash that leaves

your psyche fresh and clean. When you finally free yourself from your monkey tyrant, you can relax and begin to recover in your own private little sanctuary of serenity. I refer to this clear, agenda-free, yet focused state of mind as *non-thinking*.

Non-thinking is an easy concept to understand, but a difficult one to achieve. For many, it is a challenge to still the monkey mind. This is natural and understandable. After all, we have spent most of our conscious life moving from one branch of thought to another, talking to ourselves all the way.

Practice:

Make meditative practice a daily activity in your life. Being consistent in your practice is more beneficial than spasmodic, grueling, marathon iron man sessions.

If you find yourself too stressed to meditate, that is the exact time you should.

You will be surprised at how effective meditation is at achieving a spontaneous remission of your angst and more serious psychogenic afflictions.

The human mind is a fountain that continually bubbles forth with an inexhaustible effervescence of thought. Meditation is the great control valve.

BENEFIT-2: HEALING THE BODY

Inverted Priorities:

Our negative states of mind - angst-ridden, depression-ready, and anger prone - make us sick, and those around us recoil. With our neglect of internals, and obsession with externals, Western culture is a great breeding ground for psychogenic afflictions. We are busy outside and troubled inside.

First we give up our health to gain wealth, and then give up our wealth to regain our health.

Cognitive Karma:

There is much evidence that negative states of mind cause psychosomatic or emotionally induced illnesses. Our thoughts can be self-defeating or self-destructive. Some studies indicate that over half our hospital beds are occupied with people with not physical, but emotionally induced illnesses. Stress, overwork, lack of sleep, anxiety, fear, depression, anger, traumas, and overuse of prescription drugs take their toll. They slowly compromise our immune systems, contribute to obesity, and make us vulnerable to diseases and even an early death.

Two Fundamental Benefits:

Meditation can help heal the body by the two fundamental ways mentioned earlier: by removing negatives and adding positives. Through meditation (especially guided meditation) we can eliminate negative states of mind, and visualize positive states of health.

The Power of Suggestion:

Experiments with *placebos* have confirmed the great power of suggestion. Stage hypnotists have demonstrated this power to a comical extreme. In one dramatic demonstration of how the mind affects the body, a hypnotist put a subject in a trance, and touched an ice cube to his skin. The hypnotist told the subject that it was a red-hot coal. Blisters formed on the subject! The cells on his skin actually seemed heat damaged, as if a hot coal had touched them! In a similar but less dramatic way, our mind affects our body. The mind-body connection has been well documented in holistic health circles. Our dirty mental dishwater can bring emotional *dyspepsia*.

Conversely, our happy and healing thoughts can arrest and even reverse physical illness. Dr. Norman Cousins reportedly put his cancer into remission with humor. Such visualizations demonstrate the power of cognition.

With a little imagination we can begin to see how Taoists use meditation to overcome ennui; to unblock *chi*; and to direct life energy to different parts of the body for healing and vitality.

BENEFIT-3: DISCOVERING THE SELF:

"Know Thyself":

A central aspect of the spiritual path is a continuous sense of inquiry and quest for the truth. And the most important truth is that of the "self." As Socrates advised over 2400 years ago: *"Know thyself."*

An important use of meditation is for autognosis – knowledge of the self. This includes the apparent and hidden levels of our mental, physical, and emotional or spiritual realms. One of our first destinations in our exploration of inner space should be to sense the pneuma of our vital force. Here we will have an opportunity to uncover new facets of our self, and perhaps even do some deep-soul work. Be prepared for some uncomfortable or even disturbing self-discoveries. You may be among the walking wounded and not know it. We often suppress painful memories, and almost all of us have them.

An Important Question:

Ask yourself what your soul longs for. Listen to your mystical inner murmurings. They will give you clues for healing and transformation.

Impermanence:

Within the quietude of meditative repose, you can also begin to understand the transient nature of the self. Buddhists call this *no self* or *anatta*. We are just a transient energy bundle in time-space. Who has the courage to recognize this non-existence, much less the transformation into what we call death?

Focus on the breath and think of inhalation as the symbol of birth and exhalation as the symbol of death. This can be practiced lying down, sitting, standing, or even walking. This meditative practice can bring a great perspective on life. It has the power to allow us to see the unimportance of little things.

Our Private Chamber of Horrors:

We all have a private chamber of horrors in the catacombs of our mind. Go to it now. Look at all the vampire bats of fear hanging from the rafters. See the ghosts of the past walking around. Attend the mental monsters ball. Feel the bite of the reptiles that hide in the dark ooze of our pathologies. There is even a rack where we can torture ourselves for hours and even days with unbearably painful thoughts.

Watch fearful creatures enter the theater of your conscious, play their part, snarl and threaten, and then exit stage left. If one actor in your horror show keeps returning, it is a sign that he is trying to get your attention. And he won't let you rest until he does. Maybe he wants you to apologize or atone in some way for harm you have caused. Or perhaps he wants to remind you of a big "owie" in your heart that has never completely healed.

Use meditation to discover what hidden deficiencies and hurts require your attention, and then take care of them. In time you will be amazed at how liberated you feel. No longer will boogiemen threaten you and drain your psychic energy.

Body Awareness:

Use meditation to listen to your body. It continuously transmits and receives information. If we ignore its requests or warnings, the body amplifies the strength its message. If we continue to ignore it, the body will increase the severity of its messages. In the extreme, it will shut down major systems and even bring death in order to be heard.

BENEFIT-4: CREATING A BUFFER ZONE

Through meditation you can develop a buffer zone between you and the outside world. With steady practice, you can extend this buffer zone to your non-meditative time. This can be very useful in your quest for inner peace. Keep practicing. You will find that you are less shell shocked by the incoming rounds of enemy fire in the war of life. One day, you will be pleasantly surprised when a provocation that would normally upset you does not. It is like an incoming missile that falls a little short and explodes harmlessly away from the secure bunker of your mind.

After developing this protective barrier though steady meditation, when a psychological bomb does explode in front of you, your mental flack jacket will protect your psyche. You will not spasmodically react with panic, anxiety, or anger. Your buffer zone will insulate you so you will have time to process the action in a calm, rational way.

Ultimately you will be able to detect threats and take preemptive action by defusing ticking bombs before they explode.

Meditation will allow you to maintain equanimity under all types of stressful conditions. The many emotional tsunamis of life will not quite reach your peaceful little shore.

BENEFIT-5: INCREASING AWARENESS

Appreciation:

The object of focus here is everything and nothing. It is everything because the fully aware mind takes in everything. It is nothing because it is non-thinking (not to be confused with no-thought).

The goal is to develop a natural appreciation and joy from just being alive. This does not require intellectualizing. Survivors of near-fatal accidents or diseases know this state well. They have learned through a real life trauma or even near-death experience to appreciate every moment of this precious human life.

Presentness:

Zenists have refined this application of meditation to an art. They bypass discursive thought and become fully engaged in *presentness*. They experience the "dropping away of body and mind." This is meditation without focus on a particular object. It approaches a total, unencumbered clarity.

The idea here is being aware of thought, but not *in* thought.

Mutual Arising:

Meditative practice builds peace of mind. This means being less distracted. With fewer distractions, you will increase your awareness and concentration. With greater awareness and concentration, you will enter higher states of consciousness.

This combination of inner peace and undistracted concentration is known in Buddhism as "mutual arising" or *samadhi*. You will be amazed at how empowering and transformational this state of mind can be. Everything becomes clearer and more alive. And you become much more efficient and effective in everything you do.

BENEFIT-6: FINDING ANSWERS

During meditation, focusing on the question of how to solve a vexing problem sends it deep beneath the psychic surface and into your subconscious. Your subconscious will then go to work using its vast data bank and connections to solve the problem for you. Over time (how much time depends on the complexity of the problem), you will be surprised at how elegantly simple solutions will bubble up to your conscious "out of nowhere." Your mind becomes a lightning rod for incoming answers to your question.

Many people, including mathematicians and scientists, have had the experience of going to bed with a puzzle on their mind, and waking up with a complete answer. We have an immense database in our brain that possibly has cosmic connections that we can access with practice.

BENEFIT-7: TRANSFORMING

Programming:

A very empowering application of meditation is to program our mind with positive thoughts that bring personal transformation. After our mind is cleansed and settled by meditation, it has a clarity, access, and receptivity otherwise unavailable. This openness facilitates the introduction and retention of positive visions of who we want to be. We can make great improvements in every area of our life in this way with this visualization or imaging.

Autogenic Conditioning:

In Western psychology, the use of meditation for transforming to higher levels of performance is called *autogenic conditioning*. Professional athletes use this powerful mental technique to increase their performance by visualizing superior abilities and competitive victories. Russian athletes competing in the Olympics reportedly used this advanced technique with great success.

Self-Realization:

We can use meditation to program our mind with character-building images. We can become the person we dream of being by imprinting the image of that person deep into our psyche. Each of us has a potential that has yet to be realized.

This use of meditation for personal development is very powerful. It can transform your mind and your life in very profound ways. It is the inner fast track to self-actualization.

> Note: I use transformational visualizations daily -both in and out of meditative practice - to program my mind toward my ideal-real self.

OBSTACLES TO MEDITATION:

The most advanced practitioners of meditation, such as yogis, can remain totally focused on an object for very long periods of time. This is called *tranquil abiding*. But for the rest of us, remaining focused in mediation is difficult to do for more than a couple of minutes. There are always obstacles in the path of progress. In the rules for meditative engagement, here are some of the outer and inner obstacles to recognize, and neutralize:

OUTER DISTRACTIONS:

Lifestyle:

In this busy modern world, one of the biggest obstacles to meditating is the lack of time. However, the more your routine is filled with demanding, stressful activities, the more you need to meditate. It is a matter of priorities. First things first.

Environment:

It is difficult to meditate when you are in an environment that is noisy, unclean, unorganized, too bright, too hot, too cold, too windy, too humid, too full of people or pets, or too distracting in any way. Meditation should be practiced without straining to avoid distractions.

INNER DISTRACTIONS:

The *Monkey Mind*:

This is the most common obstacle for both new and experienced practitioners of meditation. Obsessive, burdensome, or just plain random thoughts are all impediments to mediation, and to efficient living. The reduction of this mental overhead is one of the best reasons to meditate.

With regular meditative practice, you can eventually sedate the terrorist monkey, end his blathering, and clean up his cage. But it will not be easy.

When you first begin to meditate you will discover how difficult *non-thinking* is to achieve. You will begin to realize that you have been living – maybe much of your life - in a kind of an agitated state. You will find yourself afflicted with an almost uncontrollable mental, physical, and emotional nervous energy.

When you try not to think, for a few moments you will temporarily suspend this life-long habit. But soon you will begin to naturally gravitate into thought. You won't even know it until you are well into a recollection, worry, problem, plan, or even delightful fantasy.

Physical Distractions:

It is also difficult to meditate when you have inner physical diversions such as drossiness, agitation, thirst, hunger, itches, aches, pains, heat, cold, etc. Sometimes when you try to be still, you will have a restless urge to jump up and move about. You will begin to notice little discomforts in your body. The more you try to ignore them, the more distracting they seem to get. Some teachers train students to ignore these distractions. I say scratch that itch, or shoo that fly, and get on with the meditative session without distraction. Otherwise, it is more digressive to try to overcome it. If you find yourself falling asleep when you are meditating alone, go take a nap, wake up refreshed, and restart your session. Monks exert great discipline in fighting the strong inclination to doze during long group meditations. Some even allow themselves to be struck with sticks when they nod off.

Makyo:

A *makyo* is an image or vision that appears while meditating. It can be murky and vague, or clear and specific. Do not worry. It is harmless.

ADVENTURES IN MEDITATION
MY *MAKYO* EXPERIENCE

The first time I meditated at a guided Zen meditation class I was seated on a cushion facing a wall with my eyes cast downward. I had an apparition of an indistinguishable dark inky figure. I asked the Zen master about it, and he explained that it was probably a *makyo*. (Since it had a name, I reasoned, it must be common enough that I need not doubt my mental stability - at least not for that reason.)

WHEN TO MEDITATE:

You can meditate anytime it is convenient. The question of when to meditate is almost like the question of when to sleep. The answer is when the need arises. If you feel that you are too busy, preoccupied, stressed, frustrated, worried, anxious, disagreeable, or angry to meditate, that is exactly when you should meditate.

Meditate whenever you find you have troubling thoughts, ill health, nervousness, depression, fears, financial problems, social issues, or are simply not yourself.

Meditation can always bring you back to your original prototypical self, that starting place of peace and clarity.

Meditate at the beginning of your day. This will bring you a calm, cool, efficiency to everything you do.

Meditate - even for a minute - before a demanding personal or professional event. This could be a college exam, important business meeting, social occasion, speech, medical/dental appointment, marriage ceremony, divorce court appearance, or any emotionally charged activity.

HOW LONG TO MEDITATE:

There are no hard and fast rules as to how long to meditate. This is not about adhering to a dogma or institutionalized program of any type. This is about your self-development and your sacred path. Tailor it to your needs and no one else's.

As a general guide, beginners might carve out at least 10 or 15 minutes every day to still the *monkey mind*. Affirmations can be done within 20 to 30 minutes if the mind can be settled quickly. Advanced practitioners meditate for one or two hours or more at a sitting. In retreats, adherents meditate for many hours a day over many days. They usually come out of such experiences with new perspectives on themselves and the world.

Remember this: The quality of your meditation is more important than the quantity of it.

(From the West: "*Less is more.*")

PRESCRIPTIONS:

"*If your mind is empty, it is always ready for anything. It is open to everything. In the beginners mind there are many possibilities; in the experts mind there are few.*" – Shunyu Suzuki

CONSIDER GUIDED MEDITATION:

Guided meditation sessions led by a competent instructor can be very beneficial. You will learn technique, but also feel the synergistic power of the collective.

INDIVIDUAL MEDITATIVE PRACTICE:

Meanwhile, here are nine basic steps to guide you in your individual meditative practice:

STEP-1: PREPARE YOUR OUTER WORLD

Despite its natural allure, do not try to meditate outdoors. There is always something that will distract you such as wind, cold, heat, sun, insects, people, dogs, noises, and other things. You may have a special place that is the exception to this rule. Use it if you wish as long as you are not disturbed.

Find an indoor setting that is quiet, clean, neat, darker, peaceful, and otherwise conducive to focused concentration. Check the subtleties. Does the room contain adequate ventilation? Is the temperature comfortable? Is it quiet? Is it too bright? Are there electrical fields near? Is the room free from chemicals such as those in carpets, counters, and out-gassing construction materials?

Select and design an area to be your peaceful, healing, sacred space. *Feng Shui* can be of help here.

Masters can meditate almost anywhere, but beginners need all the comfort they can get. Some people even set an alarm clock for the duration they wish to practice so as not to wonder about the time. Select a comfortable seat. Meditative cushions are available through a wide variety of retail outlets and on-line. If you cannot meditate on a cushion, just use a chair. But select one that keeps your back straight.

STEP-2: PREPARE YOUR INNER WORLD

Many teachers advise setting a regular time in your daily schedule to meditate. But if this is not possible, be flexible. Meditate any time of day or night.

Take care of any bodily needs you might have *before* starting to meditate. Do not over/under drink or over/under eat before your session. Make sure you are not too hot or too cold. Avoid restrictive clothing. Be comfortable!

STEP-3: DECIDE ON YOUR MEDITATIVE PURPOSE

Introduction:

Some teachers believe that meditation should not have a purpose, that it is an end in itself. My problem with this is that it is unnatural. Our brain is an amazing, purposeful, goal-driven, biochemical machine. It wants to have a purpose, and focus. It does not want to be in an undirected state.

Select:

Intention is very important in meditation. From the "Seven Ways to Benefit from Meditation" covered earlier and listed below, decide on the purpose of your meditation. Be specific. Then develop a mental picture of how you would think, feel, and be as an embodiment of that virtue. Here are examples for each of the seven:

1. Taming The *Monkey Mind*:

This first meditative purpose is the most important, and the most challenging. Reduce the impedance on your internal circuitry so there is less frictional heat and energy loss. Discontinue distorting and painful thoughts. Sweep out your intellectual clutter. A calm mind is a necessary prelude to all other meditative purposes. Think of your mind finally being free from all painful memories or disruptive thoughts. Visualize yourself as serene, clear, and totally attentive to the present. Stay open and present. Develop what Zenists call *the beginners mind.*

2. Healing The Body:

Picture yourself in optimal health. See yourself with such a strong immune system that you remain free from any disease including common colds and flues. Eliminate the very idea of sickness from your self-image by driving a picture of perfect health deep into your psyche.

3. Discovering The Self:

As always, start by eliminating negatives.

Take a scenic tour of yourself to discover any possible problem areas. Connect the dots of your mysterious psyche to form an image of your inner self. Do your own soul-reading. Quit shadow boxing with phantoms, and be present in the real world. Clean out the damaging residue of your past.

It takes courage to face your deepest fears, insecurities, weaknesses, grief, sorrows, mistakes, anger, rage, and regrets. It requires that you set your defenses aside. Meditation can help you find and confront these vexations to your spirit. Confront and tame your inner dragons. Fully experience them; finally come to a permanent negotiated settlement with them; and then let them go forever. Only when you complete this process will you be free to move forward and fulfill the great promise of your life.

Once you perform this psychic cleansing and free your mind from its prison, begin the joyful discovery of your inner essence. Focus attention on your inner signals that leave clues to the core of your being. Concentrate on the question: Who am I? Then let the answer or answers emerge. Think back to your earliest memories of yourself. What impressions do you have about your inner nature as a child? Ask yourself if those same traits are still with you today. Those that are can provide clues to your natural tendencies. These traits are similar to *imprints*, one of the five *skandhas* ("groups" that compose the self) in Buddhism.

You may find that you have always been logical, methodical, or even quantitative. And/or, you may find that you have always been creative, artistic or musical. Identify the larger patterns of your life. Sense the gestalt of it all. Do not immediately analyze what emerges. Just notice and witness while you are alive in the moment. Make note of what ever seems natural, consistent, and beneficial to you. These are clues to your nature. It is never too late to find yourself... in the rapture of the deep.

4. Creating A Buffer Zone:

Visualize an impenetrable, soundproof, barrier between you and the outside world. Develop a safe harbor for your senses. Make it a refuge from the madness of the world. You could visualize this as an invisible force field, a clear plastic bubble, or anything that works as an image of that which protects you. Sense that you are safe from the inevitable turbulence and air pockets of life. Feel how this buffer zone blocks out all the noise, stress, and bedlam of your world. If you meditate on this zone long enough, you will be able to re-experience most of this secure feeling when you are not meditating. This is especially useful when you are around toxic people. The calm and peace that you achieve during meditation (first purpose) will be with you again, and you will be able to handle stressful situations much better. The advantage of developing this mental buffer zone is that it will lessen the probabilities of any uncontrolled reflexive emotional responses to the provocative vicissitudes of life. Instead of getting scared or angry when being socially shot at, you will feel like the word bullets are bouncing off your shield.

5. Increasing Awareness:

Appreciation: First, develop awareness of the great privilege of simply being alive! (Just think of how many people are not.) Experience an attitude of gratitude for the opportunity to be breathing fresh air and walking on this Earth. The intent here is to generate a feeling of appreciation rather than an intellectual understanding.

Presentness: Silence your inner discursive thoughts and be fully in the moment. Meditate on no object in particular, and experience the "dropping away of body and mind." Be aware of thought, but not *in* thought. This is similar to the Buddhist concept of *presentness.*

6. Finding Answers:

If you are in a quandary about something, formulate a crisp question about it. For instance, if you are confused about your next step in life, ask where you would ideally like to be in a year. (This is similar to the divination process of the *I Ching.*) Simply meditate on this question. Take note of the way your mind begins to fill in the space between the present, and the future a year from now. Your mind will formulate the answer and the path will reveal itself.

7. Transforming:

This is a very empowering use of meditation. Chose a quality or virtue you wish to strengthen in yourself. For example, lets say you wanted to become a model of wisdom. Visualize yourself as a person who possesses great dignity, astuteness, common sense, insights, and intelligence of a profound kind. Create an image of how you would think, talk, and act as a sage. Meditate on that vision of your wise self. With repeated practice, your subconscious will interpret that vision as operating instructions. Most importantly, it will go to work making it come true. One day you will feel a sense of self-confidence and maturity that was not there before.

Use transformational meditation for any virtue you wish to embody like truthfulness, strength, loyalty, magnanimity, charity, compassion, friendliness, and love. You can also use it to enhance your mental and physical performance at a personal or professional skill.

Finally use transformational meditation it in a broad sense to develop a very positive image of you as a completely developed person.

STEP-4: ADJUSTING ATTITUDE

Maintain a good attitude about your meditative practice. It should be natural and joyful, never artificial or forced. Your motivation makes all the difference, the more natural the better. Visualize the benefits of your meditation to yourself and others.

STEP-5: ADJUSTING POSTURE

Sitting On The Cushion:

A straight posture is emphasized, especially in Zen meditation. Traditional meditation is practiced sitting on a firm cushion on the floor. If you use one, position it so that you form a tripod with your two knees and bottom. If you are flexible enough, try the half and eventually full lotus position. This is where one or both of your feet are folded up onto the opposite thigh.

Sitting On A Chair:

If being on a cushion is too difficult, just sit in a chair with a firm, straight, back with your legs perpendicular to the floor. Just make sure there are no pressure points. Your spine should always be straight. Your clothes should be loose and hang on you as they would on a rack hanger. You should never be uncomfortable or in pain. Sit straight so your mind does not become lazy.

Hands and Arms:

Just be naturally comfortable. In traditional Buddhist meditation, the left hand symbolizes wisdom and cradles the right hand, which symbolizes compassion. The thumbs touch – to complete the circle - near the vicinity of the navel. Your hands should rest gently on your lap. Your arms can be held slightly away from the body so air circulates.

Eyes:

Your eyes should be partially closed to dim the light and distractions. You could close your eyes, but not when you are tired or you will doze off. Fix your sight on a spot in front of you so your chin is angled slightly downward. Adjust your field of vision to compensate for your level of mental activity. If you are too energetic, close your eyes and lower your chin more. If you are sleepy, open your eyes more and raise your chin. The idea is to be able to clear your mind without inner or outer distractions.

Walking Meditation:

Zenists practice sitting meditation known as *zazen*, but they also do walking meditation. The posture is erect; the hands are clutched together near the end of the breastbone; the eyes are cast downward; the pace is slow and steady; and the focus is on the breath.

STEP-6: TAMING THE MONKEY MIND

No matter what the basic purpose of your meditative session, start by removing any mental obstacles you may be harboring. Take the time you need to sedate the little monkey guy. You can quiet him down by focusing on your breath, a spot on the floor, a candle, or anything that allows you to concentrate. The most traditional focus is on the breath. Concentrate on how your regular, calm breath feels as it passes through your nostrils on each inhalation and exhalation. Focus on this sensation to the exclusion of everything else.

It is natural for your mind to wander. You will see just how active and wayward it is. Just keep returning to the breath. Sometimes you will have to use your entire meditative session time on just taming the monkey mind.

As a pond is clouded by stirred up silt, so is our mind clouded from our thoughts. Calm the pond of your mind until it is crystal clear, open, and spacious. You will then find a peace like no other.

STEP-7: MEDITATING

Keep your mind clear and proceed with the purpose you selected for your meditation. Remember that the mind can only focus on one object at a time, so use this fact to avoid diversions and to stay on task. Do not give any power to digressive thoughts. Develop concentration. Keep extending the time you can stay focused.

STEP-8: RE-ENTERING

Do not suddenly end your meditation session, and jump right up. Your mind, body, and emotions are in a calm state and you do not want to shock them with an abrupt reentry. Slowly rise out of the depth of peace into the world around you. Never return with a loud noise. Although Zen centers often use a very sharp, resonant chime to signal the end of a meditation session.

STEP-9: PRACTICE

The chronicles tell that Bodhidharma, the Buddhist teacher who brought the *dharma* to China in sixth century A.D., meditated nine years while staring at a wall in his cave. Meditative practice means just that, *practice*. Repetition is important. It is like every other endeavor in life, the more you do it, the better you will be at it, and the more rewards you will receive. It does not have to consume your days or evenings. You do not have to be another Bodhidharma. But do give the practice the respect it deserves in your life. The benefits you derive will be well worth the time and effort you invest. In fact, meditation might be *the best* investment you will ever make from a time, benefit, and cost ratio standpoint. Like so many other great gifts, there is no monetary cost.

(From the West: *""Practice poses the question: "What is this?" and by doing so reminds us that what we seek is directly in front of us.""* – Diane Rizzetto)

FINAL THOUGHTS ON MEDITATION:

Please remember these five concluding thoughts about meditation:

1. Meditation has been repeatedly prescribed by some of the most respected and influential spiritual leaders and healers in both modern times and in ancient history.

2. Many millions of people have practiced and benefited from meditation for thousands of years.

3. Take time each day to meditate, even for five or ten minutes to clear your mind of troubling thoughts.

4. Take time each day to reinforce your greatest visions of yourself and your future through meditation.

5. Remember that you can meditate almost anywhere, for any length of time, at no expense. What a beautiful gift!

THE PHILOSOPHY OF TAOISM – EPISTEMOLOGY

TRUTH

DESCRIPTIONS:

"Without going outside, you may know the whole world." – Lao Tzu

TRUTH AND SELF:

Truth is the essence of Taoism. Taoists steadfastly seek the truth. And like with so many of their other efforts, they begin within. Here they have an advantage: Their essential egolessness allows them to remain objective in their search. And their search is not an academic one. Nor is their knowledge arrogant. They do not claim to corner the market on truth, as do so many religious and secular dogmatists. From the Tao Te Ching: *"The more you know the less you understand."*

Taoists seek inner truth through meditation and introspection. They question themselves. Free from denial, they plumb the depths of their inner beings to uncover both their problems and their potentials.

TRUTH AND OTHERS:

By being truthful with the self, followers of the Tao are truthful with all others. (A causal relationship that was eloquently expressed by Shakespeare.)

Taoists look for the truth from others. But they know

that appearances are deceiving. They are not fooled by surface impressions, or clever dissimulations. They understand that who people really are is a mystery that can only partially be solved over time. They wait for the truth to emerge after the awkwardness, drama, and posturing of initial encounters. They know that first statements are decoys. They wait for the second and even third issues that arise in the conversation to learn the true reason for the exchange of pleasantries.

TRUTH AND NATURE:

Taoists respect and revere the wisdom of nature. They cut through the artificialities of the man-made world, and with penetrating intuition discern the laws that explain the natural world. They seek its many gemstones of truth through observation and inference. They observe the operation, patterns, and cycles of the natural world, and infer the dynamics of its laws.

In a sense, all the subsequent topics on Taoism can be viewed as snapshots along the way to fundamental truth.

(From the West: *"Truth exists. Only lies have to be invented."* – George Braque)

PRESCRIPTIONS:

"What is meant by a "true man"? The true men of old were not afraid when they stood alone in their views."
– Chuang Tzu

DECIDE:

Do you want to see yourself as you are, or as you imagine yourself to be? Do you want to see other people as they are, or as your projection of them? Do you want to go along with the delusions and deceptions of others, or be intellectually honest and challenge them? Do you want to please others and fit in, or be genuine and perhaps be left out? Do you want to buy into the propaganda and superstitions of your time and place, or think and live with rationality? Do you want to see the world realistically, or distorted through the prisms of fear, anger, need, and desire? Do you want to seek the truth above all else, or compromise for comfort, lassitude, expediency and gain?

If your answers to the above questions were on the side of truth, next decide how *far* on the side of truth you want to be. Decide how dedicated you really are to the truth. There are personal, professional, and social situations when it is advantageous to shade the truth, or even to outright lie. Determine what effort you are willing to make, and what price you are willing to pay, for the truth. This is important to know, because you *will* be tested. There will come a time when you have to make a difficult choice. Holding to the truth may involve a significant disadvantage, or even painful hardship. It will be very tempting to take the untruthful way. Indeed, this will be your *moment of truth*.

It is easy to assume a virtue, but much harder to live it. This is the difference between ethics and morality.
Throughout history, people were willing to die for the truth. In today's win-at-any-cost, greed-distorted world, people take pride in their clever manipulation and distortion or the truth. They feel proud if they get away with deception and get the better of someone...until the inexorable law of *karma* corrects the cosmic scales of justice.

SEEK THE TRUTH:

Seek the truth in all aspects of your life. Be honest in both your inner and outer worlds. Why delude yourself in either? Listen to your mind, body, and emotions. Know your financial situation. Examine your personal and business relationships. See and hear what is really going on in your life. Question your tendency to see things only from your point of view. Sharpen your instincts. Use your built-in lie detector. Recognize distortion and dishonesty. Be aware of betrayal.

Begin a quest to find out the answers to life's important questions. Be driven by curiosity. Develop a "beginner's mind" (Very Zen). Be an amateur scientist. Gather information from valid sources. Seek expert advice. Develop your own theories. Test your hypothesis. Continuously refine your conceptions with further observations and peer reviews.

TRUTH AND CONSEQUENCES - A MORAL DILEMMA:

Think, communicate, and act truthfully. This takes not only attention and effort, but also courage. Be a model of truth. Inspire others to be the same.

Expect situations to develop where it is very difficult to tell the truth. Someone might ask you a question, the truthful answer to which would be damaging to his or her self-image or happiness. In some extreme cases, a truthful answer could also jeopardize someone's life. Two examples:

1. During World War II, Nazi's interrogated many honest people in their pursuit of Jews. For them to tell the truth would have cost many innocent lives.

2. A patient suffering a heart attack asks a doctor if he is having one. If the doctor tells the truth, he will no doubt upset the patient and worsen his condition.

What do we do in circumstances such as these?

The philosopher Immanuel Kant addressed this question, and brilliantly answered it. To paraphrase, he believed that in extreme cases such as those above, *the free choice to tell the truth does not exist.* The decision-maker is subject to extreme duress and undue influence. The situation is tantamount to having a gun pointed at their head. So the option to tell the truth has, in effect, been denied them. They are therefore relieved from the moral imperative to tell the truth. Do not of course liberally construe this ethical escape clause to shade the truth out of convenience.

(From the West: *"Adversity is the first path to truth."* – Lord Byron)

THE PHILOSOPHY OF TAOISM – ETHICS

PERSONAL RESPONSIBILITY

"*A solitary crane in winter snow needs no jewels.*" – Taoist saying

DESCRIPTIONS:

TWO WORLD VIEWS:

As we develop through life, we adopt one of two general *weltanschauungs* (world views) regarding responsibility: inward or outward. These two diametrically opposite orientations are demarcated by the thin boundary of our skin. We either go within for personal responsibility or we make others responsible.

Of course, everyone lives in both his and her inner and outer world. No one is totally independent or dependent. But we are referring here to where the individual places authority, control, and power for the important aspects of his or her life.

Taoists always look within. They take full responsibility for every important aspect of their life. Let's first look at the opposite – the "other responsible" personality.

THE "OTHER-RESPONSIBLE" PERSONALITY:

Introduction:

The other-responsible personality holds others accountable for their problems and their failures. They place primary responsibility for their important life issues outside of themselves. Here is the myth and reality of some of their statements:

The Myth: "*You made me feel bad*"
The Reality: No one can *make* anyone feel good or bad.

The Myth: "*You held me back*"
The Reality: No one can hold anyone back for long. We can either negotiate a successful resolution to a problem, or find success elsewhere.

The Myth: "*You just can't win.*"
The Reality: If the "system" is rigged against the individual, why has it worked for so many others?

The other responsible individual looks to their mates, friends, employers, social groups, and governments to in some way take care of them.

Relying on others is not inherently good or bad. We are all connected, and interdependent. But it becomes a problem when we look outward for things we should find inward.

Mentality:

What follows are some of the more common characteristics of "other responsibility" thinking:

The Blaming Mentality:

The "other responsible" individual is never at fault. They hold other people or things responsible for their misfortunes and failure. So when a challenge arises, or life takes a wrong turn, the focus of blame is on someone or something, or the ubiquitous "they."

The Victim Mentality:

Another characteristic of the "other responsible"

personality is the expectation that others will fix their problems. This is part of the victim and entitlement mentality. It is often fostered by dependency politics. Well-intentioned government programs often begin tightly focused on the truly needy. But over time they inevitably evolve into broad, bloated, scandal-ridden, money-pits. They dispense a compassion that cripples, and their "clients" become weaker, not stronger. This leads to even more dependence on the state. Hence, the program-client relationship becomes synergistic and mutually rewarding. No wonder government is like the universe - continuously expanding.

The Consumer Mentality:

The "other responsible" individual often diverts their attention from their unhappiness by over consuming. They look outward again to things that will dull their pain and senses so they won't see how they really are. Marketing specialists are very skillful at recognizing, legitimizing, developing, and pandering to every imaginable type of vain, narcissistic, "other responsible" indulgence. They are very adept at convincing us that their product or service is indispensable to our health, happiness, success, and social standing.

The Disempowered Mentality:

The "other responsible" individual often relinquishes control to an authority figure, a father figure, a spouse, or a deity. Here is the difference between the spiritual mentality and the disempowered mentality: The former comes from a position of humility, yet self-confidence. They remain in charge of their life. The latter comes from a position of enfeeblement and hopelessness. They negate their innate abilities, and become a passive spectator in their life.

Reasons:

There are three common reasons why some people shift responsibility to others:

Lassitude:

First, many people are simply lazy. They would rather let others take the lead, and then criticize them if they fail. They are not sufficiently motivated to think, plan, and take action on the important matters in their life.

Lack of Confidence:

The second reason people often shift responsibility is that they lack self-confidence. They fail to recognize or to develop their inherent potentials. This personal myopia narrows their vision and sense of possibilities. These poor souls never explore, much less discover, a fraction of their abilities. Eventually they relegate themselves to an unworthy and unsatisfying life. In an almost adolescent-like dependency, they grasp at security, content themselves with mediocrity, and doom themselves to a diminished destiny.

Attachments:

The third reason people shift responsibility is that they have formed desirous and dangerous attachments. A person can be energetic and self-confident yet still blame others for their problems if they have *attached* to them. That is to say that they have created emotional bonds that have made them needy and dependent. This is common among married and unmarried couples.

THE "PERSONAL RESPONSIBLE" INDIVIDUAL:

Taoist Mentality:

Taoists hold a diametrically opposite *weltanschauung*

(world view) as the "other responsible" personality. They take personal responsibility for all aspects of their life. They hold themselves accountable first, last, and always.

We should pause for a moment to reflect on this. At first, the notion of making oneself primarily responsible may seem obvious and even trite. But on second thought, consider exactly what this means.

Non-Blaming Mentality:

Taking personal responsibility means that Taoists do not make excuses. They do not blame anyone or anything for their problems or condition. They are stoic in their suffering, and do not cast stones.

Independence Mentality:

Taking personal responsibility means that Taoists minimize their dependency on others. They do not expect anyone to solve their problems. They do not rely on others (parents, partners, children, employers, office holders, etc.) for their personal or financial well-being. Taking personal responsibility also means that Taoists do not look to charitable organizations or the state to provide them with assistance. They are on their own.

Economy Mentality:

This simply means that they live simply. Taoists have what they need inside, so they need little outside. Without the heavy burdens of assets and liabilities, they are free to live in tune with the Tao.

Secular Mentality:

Taking personal responsibility means that Taoists do not expect some divinity or "higher power" to save them. A guru may not always be available, God may have other plans, and the universal intelligence may not even care. Taoists instinctively understand what John Hughes Holmes so aptly stated: *"The universe is not hostile, nor is it friendly. It is simply indifferent."*

Taking personal responsibility means that Taoists do not cover up problems with digressive and often dangerous palliatives. They do not rely on drugs to feel better. They do not need the latest electronic device or vehicle to be happy. They do not have to attend parties or travel to exotic environs to be entertained.

Taoists know that the understanding and cultivation of the inner self is necessary to deal with life's inevitable challenges. They take as a given that spiritual development is an "inside job." No one else can do it for them.

Taoists know that life is a continual process of transforming the limitations of the self and reaching higher levels of awareness and functionality. Taoists are true to themselves always. They are self-empowering, and self-directed. They do not weaken from loneliness or lack of support. Nor do they become immobilized by, or defensive about, the criticisms or negativity of others.

RESPONSIBILITY BEYOND THE SELF:

Taoist personal responsibility extends beyond the self. They know that each of us has the power - with our intellects and actions - to make a difference in the outer world. We have the power because of change and connectivity. *I* (change or transformation) (See "The Philosophy of Taoism – Metaphysics") is relentless. No matter what has been, this is a new day. Everything can change. Because of connectivity, one person – you or I – CAN make a difference.

Taoists have a deep love for people and our planet, and seek to protect both. This may simple mean that they make their life a work of art that inspires others to find the Tao. It may mean that they write or teach a better way of living. It may also mean protecting the environment from rapacious interests and carcinogenic industrial chemicals. Taoists know that the cycle of their life is finite – they are on this earth a relatively short time. During their journey here, they want to make life a little less painful, and a little more beautiful by living in harmony with the Tao.

(From the West: *"Life shrinks or expands according to one's courage."* - Anais-Nin)

PRESCRIPTIONS:

ASSUME COMMAND:

Take responsibility for all aspects of your life. Never delegate management of your life to anyone.

There are several good reasons for this self-reliance. First, you, no one else, is in charge of your life. Second, taking this personal responsibility will empower you. You will feel strong and independent. Third, by relying on yourself, you will not become disappointed or angry with others.

DEPOLITICIZE YOUR EGO:

The first step in building your personal responsibility is to depoliticize your ego. This means that you no longer distort information, either incoming or outgoing, to make yourself look good. This means you are honest, first with yourself, then with all others. This means you drop your defenses and take off your armor to access and heal the most sensitive areas of your being. This means that you live authentically and without pretense.

THINK AND LIVE RESPONSIBLY:

Never blame others for your failings in your life. If someone does an injustice to you, they are responsible for their actions. But YOU are responsible for how you respond to it. Your response makes all the difference.
Liberate yourself from unhealthy dependencies and unrealistic expectations. Never relinquish control of your destiny in any way to another. Always, be in control of your life and activities. Intelligent cooperation and inter-dependence is desirable and even essential. But never totally delegate responsibility for anything that is critical to you.

Continuously strengthen your personal responsibility throughout life. Have faith in yourself. Consult your inner authority. Take charge. Consider the opinions, needs, and wants of others, but make your own decisions, and live your own life. Don't become a bystander along the side someone else's parade.

GO GLOBAL:

Extend your personal responsibility beyond yourself. Think about the consequences of your actions to other people, institutions, and the environment. Ask what the impact of your specific thoughts or actions will be on the world, and what their collective net impact will be when you leave it.

(From the West: *"The price of greatness is responsibility"* – Winston Churchill)

P'U (AUTHENTIC BEING)

DESCRIPTIONS:

"The ancients understood that life is only a temporary sojourn in this world and death is a temporary leave. In

our short time here we should listen to our own voices and follow our own hearts." – Yang Chu

INTRODUCTION:

P'u translates into "rough timber", "uncarved block", and "raw silk" (*su*). P'u is our original, authentic being.

P'u is who we essentially are. It is our intrinsic, unidentifiable, unadulterated, unspoiled, nature before socialization, acculturation, and specialization. It is our simple, unassuming, child within before learning, conceptualizing, plotting, dissimulating, and strategizing. It is a strong, independent character without preconceptions, premeditations, or affectations. It is our pure potentials free from artificial influences.

SIMPLICITY:

The state of *p'u* is characterized by simplicity. There is no coveting or attaching to anyone or anything. (See "Detachment" under "The Psychology of Taoism") The writings of Lao Tzu are very explicit about this.

"Give up sainthood, renounce wisdom and it will be a hundred times better for everyone.

Give up kindness, renounce morality, and men will rediscover filial piety and love.

Give up ingenuity, renounce profit, and bandits and thieves will disappear."

- Chapter 19 of the *Tao Te Ching*:

What does Lao Tzu mean by these words? Is he really encouraging us to *not* be good, wise, kind, moral, and productive? I don't think so. In my opinion, the old master is telling us to return (See *"Fu"* under "The Philosophy of Taoism – Metaphysics") to the innocence of our original self (*p'u*). There we will find all these virtues naturally within us, instead of staking them as though they were some prey outside of us. This indirect approach is contained in the Western concept of the *hedonistic paradox.*

ANSWERS WITHIN:

P'u can be compared to the deep, quiet, intuitive wisdom of the unconscious mind. It does not rely on questionable information and shaky reasoning. It is self-contained and self-assured. In the words of Lao Tzu:

"Without going outside, you may know the whole world. Without looking through the window, you may know the ways of heaven. The farther you go, the less you know. Thus the sage knows without traveling; He sees without looking; He works without doing." - Chapter 47 of the *Tao Te Ching*:

What did Lao Tzu mean in this passage? Perhaps this:

- You are the expert on the subject of your self.
- You do not need to be told what is the right thing.
- All of life's important answers are within each of us.
- The truth is not "out there" but "in here."
- The sage consults his inner authority.
- Trust your original nature.

WESTERN PARALLELS:

The concept of authentic being was, as mentioned in the section on Chuang Tzu, of great interest to Aristotle. In fact, the teacher of Alexander the Great developed this idea in his self-realization school of ethics. He encouraged his students to identify and exhaustively develop all of their inherent potentials. This not only brings success but happiness as well. The emphasis on the proper application of *natural* abilities brings nothing but good to the individual and society.

Aristotle taught that we eventually meet with failure when we seek to be something we are not. The reason for our misguided efforts is ignorance and the lure of glamorous but often ill-suited endeavors. Of all of nature's creatures, man is the only one that tries to be something he is not. A horse does not try to be a cow. A fish does not act like a snake. But people often find themselves in ill-suited activities and occupations i.e., they are not in their state of *p'u*.

PRESCRIPTIONS:

"Open yourself to the Tao, then trust your natural responses; and everything will fall into place." - Chapter 23 of the *Tao Te Ching*:

QUESTION:

Do you ever get an uncomfortable feeling that you are estranged from yourself? That is, you are not being you. Statements such as the following often typify this strange and dangerous state: *"I don't feel right." "I am not myself today." "That wasn't the real me."*

Have you strayed far from you're your true path in life? Have you found yourself far from where you want to be? Have you even wondered if you have transmogrified into a trivial effigy of yourself?

If so, then unhinge from whoever or whatever has misdirected you. Be a freedom fighter, and liberate yourself from your captives. Take off your own chains.

Find yourself – your authentic being - before its "lights out."

REALIZE YOUR PURPOSE AND ABILITIES:

You were born into this world as unique as a snowflake. You owe it to your sacred self to protect and honor that uniqueness, to develop your potentials, and find your ultimate promise. Don't leave the magic in your bottle. What could give your life more meaning than to become who you are, and to do what you should do? And never doubt that you were given the *ability* to achieve both. You were not given the sight to see the ends without the means to get there. The two are inextricably linked. Rejoice in your singularity, discover your powers, and develop your ultimate destiny. This requires the next step.

DEVELOP YOUR INTUITION:

There is no more valuable ally in the quest for the selfhood of *p'u* than intuition. No significant other, no parent, no relative, no friend, no guidance counselor, no psychoanalyst can help you like your own inner source. Your awesome intuitive powers can slice through transient phenomena and superficial interests; delve deep into the intricate fabric of your being; connect with your soul; interpret its mystical language; and concisely communicate back to you the hidden essence of your authentic being.

Once you intuitively connect with your essential nature, you will develop a sense of confidence, and spontaneously move with ease and grace through life. You will naturally make correct choices in all situations, and become effortlessly efficient, and effective in whatever you do. You will feel self-assured, dynamic, and alive. You will form, and then achieve big dreams. Your life will become the great adventure, joy, and success that it was meant to be. Believe it!

PROTECT, MAINTAIN, ENHANCE:

Never lose touch with your authentic being. Never forget who you are. Never become so tempted by false images that you try to become someone you are not. Remember your essential self in stressful situations. Stay grounded in your authentic being, and you will never be swayed by the winds of change.

Use your intuitive powers to protect, maintain, and enhance your authentic being. Keep things simple, and simply be your self. Meditate on your pure, original self.

The next subject, *tzu-jan*, is authentic *living* - the logical extension of *p'u*.

(From the West: "*To do good things in the world, first you must know who you are and what gives meaning in your life.*" – Paula P. Brownlee)

TZU-JAN (AUTHENTIC LIVING)

DESCRIPTIONS:

"*The master observes the world but trusts his inner vision.*" – Chapter 12 of the *Tao Te Ching*

INTRODUCTION:

Tzu-jan:

Tzu-jan translates into "being such as itself" or "by itself so." *Tzu-jan* is spontaneous, unpremeditated, unconditioned, living in accord with the Tao.

P'u and Tzu-jan:

The previous subject, *p'u*, is authentic *being*; *tzu-jan* is authentic *living*. *Tzu-jan* is the natural result of *p'u*. If one holds to authentic being (*p'u*), then the result is authentic living (*tzu-jan*).

Tzu-jan and Ethics:

Ethics is about ideal conduct. Ideal conduct leads to *tzu-jan*. *Tzu-jan* leads to two ethical principles:

- To live in accord with our authentic (*p'u*) nature
- To not interfere (*wu-wei*) with the authentic nature of all others.

PREMISE:

The basic premise of *Tzu-jan* is that the Tao, as manifested in us, has an imminent, incontrovertible, intelligence. It is the final arbiter or ultimate guide. So there is no need for validations, approvals, or blessings from any external sources - scriptures, oracles, spiritual guides, high counsels, or ecclesiastical authority.

WHAT *TZU-JAN* ISN'T:

To help understand the concept of *tzu-jan*, we can study its opposite. What follows are several contrasting characteristics; what *tzu-jan* is distinctly not.

Dishonest:

Revering truth, the Taoist with *tzu-jan* is never dishonest with himself or with others. He does not ignore his inner voice or deny large parts of himself. He does not engage in self-deception or the deception of others. There is no artifice, pretense, disingenuousness, or dissimulations. There is no fraudulent high-moral "reasons" that strain credulity. There is no *spinner* or *spinee*, so nothing is spun.

Hedonistic:

The Taoist with *tzu-jan* is not hedonistic. Being true to her self, she is not seduced by corrupting outside influences that dull the mind, weaken the body, and poison the spirit. Authentic living creates a natural protective barrier against cultural contagions. Being strong, she isn't vulnerable to salacious titillations, social indiscretions, and sexual degradations. She knows that the "thrill-a-minute" mentality is an adolescent one that knows no lasting satisfaction. It just leads to a restless quest for the next novel stimulation. She knows that indiscriminate self-indulgences only lead to a disturbed mind, unhealthy body, tormented soul, and sad, wasted life.

Materialistic:

The Taoist with *tzu-jan* needs very little. Therefore, he has no need for career posturing, political pandering, popularity chasing, power grabbing, fortune accumulating, and status seeking. Heady power, prestigious positions, and Arabian Knights wealth actually have negative connotations to him. (Recall the story of Chuang Tzu's meeting with King Wen under "Detachment.") He knows that the character destroying, "means justifies the ends", blind pursuit of riches brings problematic complexity, economic indefensibility, environmental insensitivity, and moral decay.

Conforming:

The Taoist with *tzu-jan* does not conform to society's misdirected ways. She understands the transitoriness of the fads and fancies of the world, and she never develops a myopic zeal about any one or any thing.

She knows that fine fashions are passing passions. Neither however does she gain an adolescent delight in shocking, and neither does she engage in any type of social anarchy. There is respect for convention and authority, but not a slavish acquiescence to either.

WHAT *TZU-JAN* IS:

Fidelity to Tao:

Above all else, the Taoist with *tzu-jan* maintains focus on the eternal wisdom of the Tao. He seeks guidance from nature rather than from society. When the artificial socio-cultural world around him calls, he does not answer. He walks his own path. He uses his powers of induction to sense what the seasons are saying. He then uses his powers of deduction to apply that principle of *yin-yang* to effective living.

Fidelity to Self:

The Taoist with *tzu-jan* has an inner sense that she is a unique individual on a unique path. No one ever has been, or ever will be exactly the same as her. Others can advise and serve as examples, but she must be her own person, and walk her own way. So when she is at one with the Tao, she is surely her own best counsel.

The Taoist with *tzu-jan* maintains a life-long loyalty to the original self. She enjoys simple, graceful, living appropriate to every situation. It is constant fidelity to the *true* self, and respect for the true self of others that keeps her steady. Adherence to this high principle brings an assured, spontaneous, unpremeditated flow to her movements. At times, she may un-choose; she may reverse a wrong course. And she never forces (*wu-wei*) anything unfitting on her self or on others.

Simplicity:

Lao Tzu believed that the passions for sensual pleasure, wealth, and fame only bring disturbing envy, greed, and frustration. He advised us to embrace plainness and simplicity in mind and life. Taoists are on guard against the many seductive attractions, destructive digressions, and corrosive entrapments of the modern world. They protect their simple way of life and keep their mind uncluttered so the essential shines forth.

The Taoist with *tzu-jan* knows that what you *are*, is much more important than what you *own*. He maintains an inner and outer simplicity, and embodies the "less is more" philosophy. Free from ego temptations and liberated from the cogs of the commercial machine, spiritual, peace-seeking, nature-loving Taoists are rich in proportion to all the things they can do without.

Effortless:

Tzu-jan, the Tao within, has a smooth, stressless way of expressing itself. It is autonomous. No instruction or assistance is necessary to make our physiological systems work; to make a blade of grass grow; or to make the rainfall.

Taoists with *tzu-jan* do not work hard to achieve authentic living, but rather assume it as a foot does a comfortable old slipper. She is at one with the Tao of self - in a natural harmony with her individual nature. *Tzu-jan* gently leads to the essential virtues – truth, wisdom, health, beauty, tranquility, order, and simplicity.

All this does not mean that no attention is required and things just naturally fall into place. The world is full of diversions and traps. Awareness, effort, and discipline are always required to stay on the true path.

Self-Examination:

Taoists who revere *tzu-jan* know that there are many ways that one can be diverted from authentic living. So he regularly examines his thoughts, knowledge, assumptions, intentions, words, and actions. He looks for deviations from the true course, and makes corrections as a skilled mariner would on a great voyage.

He is especially interested in searching for his main weakness or flaw - the life-limiting factor. Each of us has one main deficiency that hinders our progress. He finds his, and with surgical skill, removes it from his character and life.

Self-Cultivation:

Knowing that it is rare for anyone to exhaustively develop all their potentials, Taoists living authentically continually refine their thinking, self-control, wisdom, skills, and deeds. She cultivates the finest in her self and inspires the same in others. This is a highly individualized path. We can benefit from sage advice, but each person is unique and must find the best way.

(From the West: *"Those who want the fewest things are nearest the Gods."* - Socrates)

PRESCRIPTIONS:

"Barn's burnt down – now I can see the moon." – Masahide

MAKE TIME:

If you are one of those people who are always too busy to do some "big picture thinking", ask yourself this question: *What am I busy about?*" If you are honestly making steady progress on the path to your dreams, more power to you. But if you feel estranged from yourself, or if you are caught in the go-go marathon without proportional rewards, it is time for a time out. Find a quiet place to rethink your life direction. Take a crash course in your self.

PHILOSOPHIZE:

Philosophic inquiry may seem abstract and irrelevant, but it has the power to *reset* your mind and recast your life in a much more positive and rewarding direction.

The Roman orator, Cicero, said that he tried every vice and became bored with them all. The only thing that he found consistently satisfying was philosophy.

ASK YOURSELF THESE *TZU-JAN* QUESTIONS:

Are you being you?

Are you living authentically? Are you being your true and best self, or are there aspects of you that are superficial, theatrical, disingenuous, and even destructive? Are you scripting and staring your own life, or are you a bit player in someone else's life drama? If you were now at death's door, could you honestly say that you have lived a life that was genuine?

Are you self-actualizing?

How many of your talents and potentials have you identified and developed? How much of what you could be, are you? How close are you to the Aristotelian ideal of self-realization?

What is your concept of the *ideal-real*?

Visualize your *ideal-real*. That is, imagine the best you

and your best *feasible* life. With that visual in mind, what kind of person are you intellectually, physically, emotionally, and spiritually? Where are you vocationally, financially, materially, and socially? How are you making the world a better place?

What are your limiting factors?

Look back on your life. Examine your self. Be honest. What mindset, way of thinking, personality trait, habit, weakness, addiction, or other factor has limited your progress? What has consistently tripped you up? One of the best things you can ever do for yourself is to identify this problem, and with great resolve, extricate yourself from it. It will be like unloading a great weight.

What should you cultivate to get you from where you are today to your *ideal-real* i.e., your personal *tzu-jan*?

What thoughts, intentions, feelings, activities, and efforts have been reliably effective for you? (Do more of them.) What are your great gifts? What are you really good at? What is your genius? What is the best and worst use of your time, energy, and resources? What is big and small in your life, and how do you determine the difference? How do you make decisions? What values and criteria do you use?

ESCAPE FROM THE BLACK HOLES:

Identify and immediately jettison anyone or anything in your life that is draining your energy or diverting you from your true path. They are on both sides of your skin: self-defeating internal factors, and unhealthy external factors. Examples include harmful thoughts (the most important one), emotions, activities, habits, traditions, possessions, and relationships. Make sure you remove all of your self-imposed restrictions. What follows are some targeted efforts:

CONDUCT A COGNITIVE CLEAN UP:

What thoughts, beliefs, and intentions do you hold that are time wasting, negative, and counterproductive? What mental obstacles do you need to overcome? What are your favorite fallacies and follies? What hurts do you need to heal? What relationships do you need to put in the past? Analyze the etiology of all of these mental maladies. Begin today to identify, reduce, and eventually eliminate them from your psyche.

PROTECT AND PERFECT YOUR HEALTH:

Introduction:

This is not a health book per se. However it is hard to imagine achieving its purpose - *inner peace* and *beautiful living* - without high levels of holistic health. Mind and body are intimately connected. What happens to one affects the other. So, what follows are some simple suggestions for optimal health.

Put safety first:

We often forget that great health can be wiped out in an instant. Accidents can and do happen. And no one thinks one will ever happen to him or her until it does.

Start today to put safety first. Identify and analyze the risk factors in your life. Reduce or eliminate them. There are the obvious situations that involve tobacco, alcohol, drugs, speed, height, water, fire, chemicals, tools, machinery, explosives, and occupational hazards. Then there are the not so obvious factors that include environmental carcinogens and unsafe neighborhoods.

> **ADVENTURES IN TZU-JAN (Authentic Living)**
> **THE STORY OF MY FATHER**
>
> My father was an athlete in his youth. When he was 29 years old, he ran across a street and was hit by an on-coming car. He survived because of his great condition, but he was never the same again. He limped all his life, and had many operations. All this pain and suffering because for one moment he did not put safety first.

Get adequate sleep:

Start each day with an adequate amount of sleep. If you tend to wake early, retire early. If you are sleepy during the day, find a place to take a catnap, perhaps at lunch. Naps are quite refreshing, and considerably boost your efficiency.

Exercise:

Develop an activity and exercise program that you can live with i.e., maintain over your lifecycle. Include stretch (yoga), strength (resistance), and aerobic (cardio) training. If you can't jog, walk. If you can't walk, move somehow. Remember that it is almost impossible to loose those unwanted pounds by a restricted diet alone.

Drink a balanced amount of *healthy* water:

Tap water in most cities is not totally safe. It is chlorinated to kill germs; fluoridated to prevent tooth decay; and alkalinized to reduce pipe corrosion. Some city water contains pesticides, herbicides, heavy metals, and known carcinogens. Find a source of safe and pure water. Filter it if necessary. Maintain fluid and electrolytic balance in your body.

Manage your nutritional needs:

"*To see disease first look at the diet.*" – Lao Tzu.

The management of your nutritional needs should be one of your highest priorities because it affects your entire well-being every moment of your life. Because each of us is a unique bio-chemical factory, you will have to find your own optimum diet. Ideally, have your blood, and even saliva and hair tested for nutritional imbalances. Meanwhile, here are some general guidelines:

Smart dietary choices: Buy fresh, *organic*, unprocessed fruits, vegetables, seeds, nuts, brown rice, whole grains, and soy products.

Things to avoid: Minimize or eliminate altogether the consumption of meat, dairy, sugar, artificial sweeteners, chemical additives, alcohol, hydrogenated products, processed products, and genetically engineered food (Frankenfood). This might be challenging, but it is necessary to good health.

Cooking: In general, the less you process and cook food the better. The one exception is tomatoes. Cook them in some olive oil to better release the cancer-fighting *lycopene*. Microwaves can alter the chemical composition of food. Use other methods to cook. Also, never microwave in plastic containers. Carcinogenic chemicals in the plastics are released into the foods.

Lipids (fats and oils): Oils should be the least refined ("cold-pressed) polyunsaturated vegetable variety with a high HDL to LDL ratio. Be careful of elevated LP (a). It is a significant marker for heart disease. Limit total caloric intake from lipids to no more than 20-25%. Avoid all animal fats, especially grilled ones.

Carbohydrates: Eat complex carbohydrates that release energy at a more constant level rather than those that shock your body and hijack your immune system.

Proteins: Reduce or eliminate your intake of animal sources of protein. Increase your protein intake from soy products such as tofu and tempeh.

Vitamins and Minerals: It is usually difficult to determine if the food you are eating really contains an adequate supply of nutrients. Our soil has been depleted. Crops are often picked prematurely. Vitamins and minerals are lost in shipping, storing, and processing. And vital enzymes destroyed in cooking. Try to buy whole organic foods. Consider taking *natural or organic whole food* supplements. If you are on a vegetarian diet, supplement with Vitamin B-12.

MAINTAIN A HEALTHY EMOTIONAL STATE:

When the mind and the body mate, emotions are their child. And this child can be healthy or sick. What we think determines how we feel. So learn cognitive control and mental mastery.

How can you maintain *Tzu-Jan*? How can you live authentically, if you have a troubled mind and heart?

Manage your thoughts and situations to minimize stress, and maximize inner peace (See "Inner Peace" under the "Philosophy of Taoism – Ethics.") Stress throws your physical systems off balance. It makes you inefficient, ill at ease, and unable to enjoy life. More importantly, stress ages and slowly kills you. Stress compromises your immune system by damaging the lock and key mechanisms of your T-cells. So, you not only become vulnerable to common cold and flue viruses, but also to more serious diseases such as heart attacks and cancer.

Identify the situational and chronic stressors in your life. Either come to healthy terms with them, or move away from them, even if it requires making personal or financial sacrifices.

Removing stress from your life really is a matter of life or death.

Find the way to consistently make healthy choices unencumbered by fear, insecurity, guilt, greed, and cultural pressures. Find a way to live each day free from any anxiety, worry, or fear. Be diligent in protecting your inner peace. Become the master, not the slave of your passions. Control your desires. Identify and avoid the innumerable traps and entanglements of the world. Forget impressing others. Be free of pretense. Give up trying to be everything. Resign as the self-appointed CEO of the universe. Opt out of the endless chase. Keep it simple. Find yourself. Make peace with life.

RIGHT SIZE:

In the West, we never seem to have *enough*. We always want more of everything. Live simply and you will be much less troubled. And others will attack you less.
Take a good look at your balance sheet of assets and liabilities. Use this test to keep or eliminate assets: Do they have a <u>future</u> value to you? Be honest with yourself. Ask when the last time you used each of the things you have. If it has been a long time, consider selling, donating, or disposing of them. Then organize the remainder of your possessions. Next, eliminate all "bad debt", that is liabilities that are associated with a depreciating asset. Pay of the debts that have the highest carrying cost (usually interest rate) first.

SELF ACTUALIZE:

Do you dare to be your true self? Do you dare to

discover and follow your own true nature? Go beyond popular images. Visualize a different and higher life. See yourself developing all of your potentials. How close are you to living that way? Listen to your ultimate authority – that voice within. Discover your potentials, and exhaustively develop them. As the Japanese dictum *masaka* instructs, find your true purpose, and make its realization your highest priority.

Courageously be your best self.

Be fully alive. Live authentically, beautifully, and successfully. Become the charioteer of your life instead of a spear-carrier for someone else. Build your own monument of greatness instead of laying stones in someone else's building. Astonish yourself with your success.

LEAD BY LETTING:

The parent, administrator, manager, or spiritual guide with a deep understanding of *P'u* and the spirit of *Tzu-jan* leads others by letting them grow and develop their best qualities. This is necessary to personal self-realization.

Be that enlightened leader that has the sagacity to know when to encourage, guide, remove obstructions, and even step aside to let others grow and develop along their unique spiritual and worldly path.

(From the West: "*People living deeply have no fear of death.*" – Anais Nin)

WU-WEI (NON-DOING)

"*The gentlest thing in the world overcomes the hardest thing in the world. That which has no substance enters *where there is no space. This shows the value of non-action. Teaching without words, performing without actions: that is the Master's way."* – Chapter 43 of the Tao Te Ching

DESCRIPTIONS:

INTRODUCTION:

***Wu-wei* is a very core concept in Taoism.**

It is difficult to overemphasize its importance. At times in the teachings, it almost becomes synonymous with the way.

THE CONCEPT:

Translation:

***Wu* translates to *non* or *not*. *Wei* translates to *doing* or *forcing*. *Wu-wei* is *non-doing* or *not forcing*.**

Wu-wei is not...

- thinking that nothing matters
- *absolute non-action*
- always being passive
- adopting an insincere insouciance
- nihilism (nothingness)

Wu-wei means not taking action that is...

- obsessive compulsive
- hostile and aggressive
- disruptive to the natural order of things
- divorced from one's correct and natural propensity
- going to result in more harm than good
- in an unthinking, robotic manner

- based on a need for acceptance
- out of fear, guilt or intimidation
- one which force feeds anyone anything
- to curry favor with a person, group, or culture
- to conform with some man-made orthodoxy
- motivated by *any* premeditated, artificial, inappropriate, narrow egocentric desires and motives

Wu-wei means...

- emptying the mind, or achieving *no-mind*
- letting things unfold according to their natures
- doing only what is necessary to complete things
- acting unconsciously and instinctively
- acting economically, without waste
- achieving worthy goals using natural forces
- creating more results
- using the least time, problems, effort, and resources
- living a harmonious life in accordance with the Tao

In Summary:

Wu-wei is such perfectly timed, naturally appropriate, effortless action that it *seems* like non-action. It is being so "right on" that there is no need to examine the correctness or purity of intentions, interests or plans. It is living with a non-conscious purity of virtue, efficiency and effectiveness.

The Missing Link in the West:

Wu-wei is deceptively powerful and universally applicable. By contrast, it diagnoses a serious Western affliction, and then offers a cure. It is one of the best-kept secrets for achieving frictionless personal, and professional success.

The understanding, application, and consequential rewards of *wu-wei* have been missing in the West because it is counter- intuitive and counter-cultural to us. We are trained to set bold goals, to *take aggressive action,* and to use force if necessary to achieve success regardless of the immediate or cosmic consequences. This bias to action is cliché. We hear remarks such as: *"It is better to do something than nothing at all."* Another frighteningly common statement is: *"I'll do whatever it takes."*

Westerners are not trained to perceive when it is wise to step back and to let nature take its course. Passivity is anathema to us. It is far too *yin.* We sedulously avoid non-action despite the fact that there are countless situations that call for us to just leaving things alone. Why is this? What follows are five possible reasons:

POSSIBLE CAUSES OF WESTERN *BIAS TO ACTION*:

Ignorance:

We are not educated to understand, much less appreciate, the wisdom of natural flow, the delicate interdependence of our world, the subtleties of situations, and the risks of intrusiveness.

Physiology:

Our endocrine system can instantly turn our body into a fight or flight machine. Unfortunately, our mistaken interpretations of situations cause us to get hot when we should chill. Our endocrine systems prepare us for drama and trauma whether the threat is real or not. Once on, we have a bias to action or physical momentum that is difficult to control and attenuate.
This has much to do with the *amygdala* in the limbic system of our brain.

Emotionality:

Contrary to popular belief, self-preservation is not the strongest drive. The preservation of the self is often second to the preservation of the *concept* of self. People have often died throughout history in order to preserve their honor and beliefs. On a less dramatic level, we often inappropriately act out to maintain or assert our self-image.

Ambition and Greed:

The question "What do people want?" has often been succinctly and accurately answered in one word: "More." We have difficulty leaving things alone because we are conditioned since birth to endlessly gain wealth and position without restraint.

Psychosocial Forces:

Our family, friends, community, and culture - especially work culture - often promote a great bias to action. In the West, who ever wins praise, promotions, or rewards for *not* acting? How often does an employer recognize and reward an employee for *resisting* the call for action? How often have you heard the foolish, macho statement: "Do something, anything, but take action."

COMPARISON:

To better understand *wu-wei*, below are two tables that contrast movement away from, and toward, *wu-wei*. The "Toward" table could be a descriptive of the *Man of Tao*.

SIGNS OF MOVING AWAY FROM *WU-WEI*
Focus on the self (narcissism)
Subjectivity and bias
Good for narrow personal interests
Always doing
Dualistic, conceptualized, divisive thought
Sectarian, slanted view
Troubled thoughts and chronic anxiety
Adherence to ridged rules, dogmas, and structures
Obsessive focus on planned outcomes
Behavior locked into a plan or other expectations
Doing *whatever it takes* to get the job done
Interventions that do more harm than good
Force first
Wasteful consumption of time, energy, and resources
Excesses and deficits in action and possessions
Confused, slow, struggle with change
Highly competitive, win-lose approach
A narrow, fixed, symmetrical, aesthetic concept
Achieve the goal on the bleeding edge at any cost
Frustration and fatigue at being in conflict with the Tao
Intolerance for unanticipated outcomes
Limited to narrow interests in life

SIGNS OF MOVING TOWARD *WU-WEI*
Focus on the Tao
Objectivity and impartiality
Greater good for all humanity
Simply being
Non-dualistic, non-conceptualized thought (very Zen)
Non-aligned, balanced view
Mental placidity and emotional calm
Freedom from contrived and unnecessary limitations
Attention to the present flow of things
Behavior appropriate to current situation
Doing just the right thing, at right time, in right way
Sometimes doing nothing, just leaving things alone

| Force as a last resort |
| Conservation of time, energy, and resources |
| Buddha's middle way and Aristotle's Golden Mean |
| Spontaneous and appropriate response to change |
| Non-competitive, win-win approach |
| Aesthetic including the imperfect and asymmetrical |
| Recognition that some things are not worth the costs |
| Joy of being in harmony with the flow of the Tao |
| Acceptance of the reality of outcomes |
| Alive to the totality and richness of life |

WU-WEI AND CH'ANG

The entire idea of *wu-wei* is to let *ch'ang* (See "The Philosophy of Taoism – Metaphysics") do its work. Essentially *wu-wei* means the non-interference and cooperation with *ch'ang*.

Now let's consult the two founders of philosophic Taoism for their thoughts on its central principle of *wu-wei*:

LAO TZU:

Lao Tzu believed that our best relationship to the world is to let it take its natural course. He emphasized this minimalist approach in personal affairs (let the Tao lead) as well as in government (let the people be.) Examples of both from follow:

"The Master arrives without leaving, sees without looking, achieves without doing a thing." – Chapter 24 of the *Tao Te Ching*

" *"When the Master governs, the people are hardly aware that he exists…..The Master doesn't talk, he acts. When his work is done, the people say: "Amazing: we did it all by ourselves." "* – Chapter 24 of the *Tao Te Ching*

The wisdom of this principle could greatly benefit both our over-stressed lives, and our over-zealous lawmakers. We all have a penchant for rushing in to "fix" things with well intentioned, but unwise, initiatives. Lacking perspective and oblivious to the broader and longer-range consequences of our actions, we are quick to make repairs. They often turn out to be not only enormously costly, but also ultimately counterproductive, and even destructive.

CHUANG TZU:

Chuang Tzu was critical of Confucianism. It was not because he disagreed with its finer principles such as *jen* (humanity), and *yi* (justice), but rather because he felt they were too constraining. He unequivocally denounced ridged institutionalized dogmas. He believed that such structures leave the individual ill prepared for unstereotypical situations not covered in our traditional norms.

Chuang Tzu inveighed against letting ones categories harden into immutability. The strict reliance on doctrine and rules weakens the capacity for independent thought and discretion when the situation doesn't neatly fit our preconceived categories. Instead, *Chuang Tzu* emphasized living with the principle of *wu-wei*, *which* allows flexibility and creativity in every situation, no matter how far removed from our past experience.

At the individual level, *Chuang Tzu* advocated that the man of Tao follow the precept of *wu-wei*. With the way of non-action, he lets things take their natural course and becomes one with the Tao. Differences between thinking and acting dissolve. (Like a Zen archer.) This brings a personal serenity that the Chinese call *Ying ning*.

At the state level, Chuang Tzu emphasized *wu-wei* in

the governance of states. He criticized the way leaders took a one-size-fits-all approach and overlooked the precious uniqueness and originality of the individual. Since no leader, however intelligent and knowledgeable, could ever begin to know what is right for each human being, the wisest course of action is to let the citizenry choose what fits them. No one else can ever know what is right for another. Instead of making assumptions and generalizations, and forcing square pegs in round holes with policies and rules, he counseled a tolerance for individuality, and advocated lassie-faire rule. Said *Chuang Tzu*:

"The wise man, then, when he must govern, knows how to do nothing. Letting things alone, he rests in his original nature. He who will govern will respect the governed as he respects himself. If he loves his own person enough to let it rest in its original truth, he will govern others without hurting them."

What conflict and damage could be avoided in our world if government and business leaders deeply understood and sincerely applied the spirit of these words?

WU-WEI AND NATURE:

Wu-wei also means not interfering with natures' way. However, there are countless ways we arrogantly disregard this truth. Here are two general categories of our folly:

Hijacking the Healing Power of Nature:

Nature has a way of healing. However, the Western medical-pharmaceutical complex believes they know better. They often do more harm than good with very expensive, high-tech, immune system compromising, invasive procedures with horrible, disfiguring side effects. There have actually been cases where patient death rates in hospitals have *decreased* when doctors were on strike. Data indicates that hospitals are hazardous to your health because of mistakes in drug prescription and treatment. Infections abound. In "digital death" medical staff enter one too many digits into intravenous machines and thereby ensure a massive overdose to the patient. Hospitals can be hazardous to your health!

Creating the Poison and Destroying the Antidote:

Nature has a way of keeping balance in the environment. However, man's arrogant, myopic, greedy, rapacious, interests have led to an indiscriminate destruction of natural habitats and a pollution of pristine ecologies. The result is ironically *karmic*. We generate chemical, industrial, and radiological wastes that cause cancers, and simultaneously destroy the rainforests that contain their cures.

MARTIAL ARTS:

The efficacy of *wu-wei* when it faces its opposite can be witnessed dynamically in some of the martial arts. *Wu-wei* is the basic philosophy behind such venerable defense systems as classic judo and *aikido*. With a minimum of effort, a defendant can turn an attackers force and momentum against him.

IN SUMMARY:

Taoists believe that we are afflicted with a compulsion to do too much, to overkill. Their antidote of *wu-wei* is to think, act, and live peacefully, effortlessly, and harmoniously with the Tao.

(From the West: *"Nature cannot be commanded except by being obeyed."* - Francis Bacon)

PRESCRIPTIONS:

"Who can wait quietly while the mud settles? Who can remain still until the moment of action?" – Chapter 15 of the *Tao Te Ching*

SEEK BALANCE:

A literal interpretation of the concept of *wu-wei*, could very easily lead the devoted Taoist to never plan, organize, set goals, or strive for results. In its purest sense, we would never think ahead or hold any premeditation. We would be unprepared every moment, always surprised and left to react spontaneously.

In my opinion, this is an extreme position that totally nullifies the goal-seeking powers we all possess, and ignores the advantages of our human ability of forethought. We all possess left and right brain hemispheres with rationalistic and intuitive powers respectively. We are born with both the ability of rationalistic preconception and of intuitive improvisation for a good reason - to use them both simultaneously and synergistically.

So, seek an appropriate balance between doing too little and too much in all areas of your life. Remember that many of the problems in the West result from doing too much. Determination in the right place can push many noble efforts to a successful conclusion. But forcing people or things is generally counterproductive. Be mindful of the immediate and subsequent consequences of what you do. Exercise appropriate restraint. Adopt a laissez-faire attitude toward the way of nature. Let the Tao do its magic.

QUESTION YOURSELF:

How good things would be, if we lived with *wu-wei*. Do

not force. The next time you find yourself struggling with someone or something to make it fit your preconceived ideas, ask why it is such an effort. Ask if there is a good reason to persist. Are you fighting ignorance, disease, poverty, injustice, or evil? (Be careful not to rationalize here.) Or are you fighting to protect your image as the self-appointed expert on everything?

If you find that there is no good reason to persist to use force, then there is a good reason *not* to. You might be going against the best interests of yourself, others, and nature. Remember the Taoist concept of *wu-wei* (not forcing, not interfering) when you encounter resistance and trouble disproportionate to the cause. Step back and get the broad perspective. Analyze what is happening. Put your ego aside. Try letting people and things take their natural, pure, and peaceful course. Remember *wu-wei* in all aspects of life. What follows are several general applications of *wu-wei*:

DO NOT FORCE THOUGHTS AND BELIEFS:

Avoid Ego Entrapments:

Never fall victim to the lure of applause and fame. Avoid all polemics and unnecessary verbal roughness. Quit jockeying for ideological supremacy. Your character will become disfigured by such senselessness.

Avoid Inappropriate Ideologies:

Don't force ideas on yourself. Be wise enough to avoid wasting your time and resources on ill-conceived personal, business, and social movements.

Don't force ideas on others. A once said: "*He who is convinced against their will, is of the same opinion still.*" How many lives have been lost in forcing religious (Christian and Islamic crusades) and political (fascism and communism) ideologies on huge populations?

Question, Test, and Refine Your Most Cherished Beliefs:

Our understanding of ourselves, much less the world, is very limited and questionable. Develop and apply your thoughts and beliefs for yourself, but continually test and refine them in the laboratory of life. Be flexible in their application and open to changes and alternative conceptions. When there is ample proof of a clearly, and consistently better way that is not in your ideology, be flexible enough to assimilate that better way. This is the essence of what the Japanese call *kaizen* – continuous improvement – an extremely powerful concept.

Note: In my opinion, the titanic political struggle in the West between "conservatives" and "liberals" indicates how primitive we still are. If there were such a thing as Taoist politics, I suspect it would be liberal in trying out new ideas to see if they had merit. It would also be conservative in preserving of all of the proven good things that have survived the test of time.

DO NOT FORCE ANYTHING INTO YOUR BODY:

The Quality of Food:

Few of us raise our own food. It is the large corporations in the agri-business that produces our food en masse. They use genetic engineering, pesticides, herbicides, growth hormones, cosmetics, and preservatives to create, ship, store, prepare, display, and sell it. The result is that the produce we are eating is the dead shell of food, not fresh, live food teaming with vitamins, minerals, and enzymes. The milk we are drinking and the meat we are eating contain the antibiotics and growth hormones pumped into our cattle. (Ever wonder why girls are entering puberty and having babies at earlier and earlier ages?)

Identify what is in the food you eat. Read labels. If you cannot pronounce it, become concerned. It is probably there for corporate interests, not for your health. These foreign substances include chemicals that compromise your immune system, undermine your health, and generate diseases - including cancer. Our poor diets have contributed to autoimmune diseases including fibromyalgia, rheumatoid arthritis, and diabetes. Many are now suffering from multiple-chemical sensitivity.

Remember *wu-wei* when you eat. Do not force *anything* on your body. There would be less proton pump inhibiting drugs sold if we would put less in our body that ricochets back up.

The Quantity of Food:

What kills people in poor countries is too little food. What kills people in rich countries is too much. Obesity is pandemic among both children (even preschoolers) and adults in the *first* world. We have created a killer culture (no longer confined to America) that combines the worst energy input-output condition. We eat large quantities of adulterated and processed junk food, and then lead very sedentary and stressful lives.

There is no magic bullet to losing weight. You must simply take in less energy than you consume. You must proportion your calorie input to be consistently and comfortably less than your calorie output - without compromising your mental, physical, or emotional health.

Everyone assumes that this is an iron man challenge that requires Herculean effort. Not true. If you educate yourself on nutrition and intelligently plan meals, with a little discipline, you can comfortably lose weight *over time*. The key is to do it incrementally, a bite at a time. Reduce a small number of calories from your diet by eliminating something superficial each day. But do this *every* day. Transition from a SAD (Standard American Diet) to one that will empower you.

DO NOT FORCE CONSUMPTION:

Our great institutions condition us from birth to desire certain products, services, entertainment, and lifestyles. Question this programming. Do you really want to force these things into your life? Are you better off with them? Do they strengthen or weaken you personally, financially and socially? Could you be happier and healthier living a simpler lifestyle? (See "Detachment" under the "Psychology of Taoism")

DO NOT FORCE RELATIONSHIPS:

You can never compel compatibility where it does not naturally exist. Never force yourself on anyone, and never force yourself to stay in a personal or business relationship that is fundamentally flawed. Never grasp and try to hold on to people. Never try to make someone like or love you. As the Zen proverb states: *"The bird of paradise does not alight on the hand that grasps."*

Remember the acronym F.I.T. - Find Intelligent Togetherness. Be your best self, and follow your best dreams. Then if someone is attracted to you, it will be for the right reasons, not based on false first impressions. Always be honest and authentic with yourself and others, and encourage them to be the same with you.

DO NOT FORCE WORK:

Identify where you are forcing yourself to do things that might be incongruous with your fundamental nature. Question your conceptions of what you should do or be. Ask yourself if your work is your choice based on correct fit, or is it an accident of proximity, convenience, or opportunism. Think for yourself, and listen to your inner voice. This is especially true for the Type-A overachieving personalities. Your workplace can and should be a stimulating, fulfilling, enjoyable, and profitable way for you to spend your waking hours. If it is not, do not force yourself to waste more of your life.

ADVENTURES IN *WU-WEI*
THE STORY OF THE MAIL CARRIER

A woman once told me she hated her job as a mail carrier. When I suggested she find more satisfying work, she said she *had to* work another 12 years at this job to build her pension. It was mind-boggling to me that someone would stay in a job they hated for another dozen years when there are so many other options in our society.

DO NOT FORCE CHILDREN:

Most children, in whole or in part, start their life being instinctual, intuitive, imaginative, happy, and natural. Parents, teachers, religious leaders, peers, and society continually force them to be someone else. The result is that these beautiful beings begin to lose their sense of self, their capacity for individual discretion, and their spontaneity, creativity, and joyfulness. We break their will and force them to conform to our prison-like molds. We transmogrify them into pitiful imitations of what they once were. We kill the kid to get the clone.

Our youth certainly should receive guidance and boundaries. They need and search for limits. However, within the healthy confines of societal norms, give them the freedom and latitude to develop in their own way at their own pace. Do not force them to be something they are not, or impose a foreign tempo on them.

Make healthy food available, but don't force a child to eat. It may be incompatible with their psychological condition or digestive systems. We are all intelligent and individual chemical factories. Who knows better than they what they need at any given moment?

Never force a child into someone else's arms, or force them to show affection even to a close relative. Children instinctively know who is right and who is not right for them. To ignore this is to disrespect the Tao of persons. Forcing someone on them is to diminish their sense of self, and to possibly precipitate a developmental aberration.

DO NOT FORCE THE UNNATURAL:

Do not force your mind and body to defend itself against its environment. Avoid stressful people and situations. Researches have found that stress interferes with the effective operation of the immune system, especially the T-Cells. Avoid toxic air, sound, water, heavy metals, chemicals, and every other type of pollutant and carcinogen. This includes an amazing range of hazards from the buzz of your overhead lights, to the metal in your fillings.

Apply *wu-wei* to the Earth. Recognize that nature, including mankind, has a delicate organic balance. Do not force the unnatural on the natural. The consequences are chilling. The thoughtless exploitation and industrialization of the planet has led to a rise in the incidence of cancers with the proliferation of agricultural and industrial chemicals, global warming, and the loss of many species and thousands of acres of rain forests.

Think about your relationships with the Earth before you force your will upon it. Develop and live an ecologically symbiotic and sustainable lifestyle.

IN SUMMARY:

Remember the importance of *wu-wei*. Apply the recommendations presented in this section. This is challenging in our pugnacious, acquisitive Western culture.

Remember to not force things on your psyche, body, or spirit; to not force relationships with incompatible people; to not force square pegs in round holes; and never interfere with the healthy development of children, or adults for that matter. A certain amount of guidance may be appropriate at times, but then let people and things take their natural, pure, correct and peaceful course.

Also remember that *wu-wei* doesn't mean never acting. There is a time and place for everything. *Wu-wei* includes taking action, but doing so in the most natural and totally appropriate way in harmony with the Tao.

(From the West: "*God grant me the serenity to accept the things I cannot change, Courage to change the things I can, and Wisdom to know the difference.*")

ADAPTABILITY

"*The hard and stiff will be broken. The soft and the supple will prevail.*" – Chapter 76 of the *Tao Te Ching*

DESCRIPTIONS:

FLEX IN THE FLUX:

The Tao is dynamic so everyone and everything is embraced in endless change. Our survival and progress depends on how we adapt to this change.

At one time or another, we are all mugged by reality. Can you recall a time when your expectations, hopes and dreams about a personal or professional future were dashed? Consider the people and nations that are at one time allies, then enemies, and then allies once again.

So with an acrobatic versatility, Taoists become skilled at adaptation. They understand that what is elegantly fitting at one time and place may be totally inappropriate at another. What is helpful this year might be harmful next year. First sooner is better and then later. Nearer is desirable and then farther. More and then less. This way and then that. And so goes the interplay of *yin* and *yang*.

Taoists are spontaneous, flexible, and creative in what they do. He is a master at effective extemporization that maintains harmony with the Tao and balances his life. He continuously seeks a harmonic convergence with the forces and cycles of nature. He remains open and tuned to the truth of the reality that unfolds before him. He is undisturbed by changes in people and situations, and are facile in adjusting to new circumstances. He is a master at intuitive improvisation. He knows that every situation requires a balanced and unique response. He is facile with unstereotypical responses.

Taoists are flexible in their methods while being uncompromising in their values. If there are two ways of doing something, she will take the way most in tune with the Tao. That way is naturally suitable to the circumstances. The means may change, but not the important ends. She intuitively chooses the way that achieves the greatest good, and simultaneously does the least harm for the given conditions.

There are times when action of some type is necessary to restore balance. For some circumstances, the best action is gradual and gentle. For others, it is rapid and violent. But always, it is appropriate.

QUESTIONING:

Taoists do not acquiesce to dogma and blindly follow orthodoxy. He is empirical. He tests his beliefs in the real world. Every one and every thing can be the subject of critical examination. You might say that he has a quintessential scientific objectivity. So he does not base his thoughts and actions on the word of some priest, book, or higher power. He makes observations, acquires evidence, seeks truth, and trusts his inner sense.

NATURAL PROBLEM-SOLVING:

While always seeking inner peace, Taoists are not afraid of conflict. She knows that some level of disagreement is inevitable because of diverse interests, divergent directions, and dynamic rates of change. When entire platoons of unexpected problems come at her, she just lines them up single file, unmasks them, and deals with each, as she is ready. She is a creative problem-solver, and alert to natural solutions that lie hidden within the problem.

Taoists never settle for superficial fixes. He gets to the heart of the problem. He is resourceful in finding unstereotypical resolutions to complex issues.

IMPEDIMENTS:

Why isn't everyone adaptable? Why is it that some people can easily adjust to new circumstances and others remain locked in old patterns? What follows are a few of the main reasons we fail to adapt to change:

IMPEDIMENT-1: PAST CONDITIONING:

Wouldn't it be irrational to wear your summer clothes in the winter? Of course this is a silly lack of adaptation. Yet we do something similar to this with certain situations in our life. We use yesterday's solutions for today's problems. One of the main reasons for this inexplicable behavior is powerful past conditioning. This programming often contains strong emotional overtones. It comes from our parents, siblings, relatives, friends, teachers, clergy, role models, mentors, and even fictitious characters.

During our early training, especially from birth to four years old, we develop experiential-based neural pathways that influence our thoughts and behaviors all through life. These pathways turn into expressways through the process of *myelination* where a fatty substance called *myelin* forms over our axons (the output side of our neurons). This insulator allows neural impulses to move more rapidly. Although the *plasticity* of our brain allows for neural change, our stereotypical patterns of response are hard to break.

If we steadfastly hold to our early conditioning and do not adapt to the new situations that continually unfold in front of us, sooner or later we will become casualties of our new realities. If we allow ourselves to become mindless automatons with unchanging instructions, we won't employ alternative tactics and strategies that accommodate changed conditions

IMPEDIMENT-2: PHYSIOLOGICAL DAMAGE:

Doctors prescribe anti-depressants to traumatized patients for a good reason. When we experience a trauma such as a serious health problem, injury, infidelity, great financial loss, or death of a loved one, certain neural pathways become damaged. The meds help the patient function during the period of neural repair, which can be up to a year. Patients, who, for whatever reason, do not fully repair, lose some functionality. They have difficulty adapting to the new reality. They can't seem to "get over it" and "turn the page."

IMPEDIMENT-3: FALSE PRIDE:

A hidden reason why so many of us fail to adapt new and better ways of thinking and living is false pride. Our spouse, relative, friend, enemy, rival, etc. (fill in the blank) discovers a better way, and we ignore it or even denigrate it.

The reason is because it originated from them, and we do not want to credit them for it with the sincerest form of flattery – imitation. Of course, it very often does not originate with them. They adopted it from someone else. As the saying goes: *"There is nothing new under the sun."*

PRESCRIPTIONS:

BE AWARE:

To improve your ability to adapt, become aware of the points made in the above descriptions. To review:

- Always sense the moving sands of time and the inevitability of change. Be aware of the continual shifts in the human, material, and environmental conditions around you.

• Analyze your past conditioning to determine if it is impeding your progress in any way. Modify or completely eliminate any burdensome patterns.

• Be mindful of how the emotions stored in your *amygdala* can work against you. Try to remember the physiological damage of fried neurons when you experience a trauma.

• Eliminate false pride. If someone finds a better way, graciously credit him or her, and consider adopting the improvement.

BE FLEXIBLE IN MEANS AND BE FIRM IN ENDS:

Remember that adaptation does *not* mean that you surrender your will, give up your values, goals, and activities, and blindly acquiesce to the forces and changes within and around you.

It *does* mean that you *stay tuned* to the Tao, develop a facile mind, decipher the nature of change, observe the patterns, and modify your behavior to best preserve, protect, and serve your finest ideals.

Learn to re-route your travels without compromising your destination. Sometimes the shortest distance between two points is *not* a straight line. Like a skilled mariner, there are times when you must divert from your true course to avoid trouble ahead; times when you must button down the hatches and wait out a storm; and other times when you must simply stop and drop anchor for a while (*wu-wei*). To proceed straight ahead is to invite disaster. There are also times when it is wise to hoist sail and catch a wind; to move with the flow of a fortuitous current; or to re-navigate to a new passage. Most importantly, always remember your destiny in the sea of life, and your current bearing relative to it.

BE CAUTIOUS:

Amid all this advice about adapting, it is important to remember that there are times when you should *not* adapt. To adapt to a situation that is wrong for you is foolish and retrogressive. Your most trusted relationships, or your secure surroundings could change for the worst over night. To adapt to them would be a mistake. Know when to hold and when to fold. Move away from the destructive rapids in the stream of life. Steadfastly maintain your independency of thought. Think critically. Seek the truth in all situations.

Remember that it is always easier to stay out than to get out.

(From the West: *"The art of progress is to preserve order amid change, and to preserve change amid order."* - Alfred North Whitehead)

SAN PAO (THE THREE TREASURES)

DESCRIPTIONS:

From Chapter 67 of the *Tao Te Ching* comes the *San Pao* or "Three Treasures." As with so many of the chapters in this venerable book, the translations differ widely. But below are the generally accepted meanings of Chapter 67. I can add little to them. They speak well for themselves.

1. Mercy, compassion, or love that fosters courage. (Biblical analog: Love casts out fear.)

2. Moderation, economy, or simplicity in thoughts,

words, and actions that fosters generosity.

3. Modesty, humility, patience, or accepting things the way they are that fosters leadership (*wu-wei*).

PRESCRIPTIONS:

Visualize how you would be if you internalized the *San Pao* in your character.

- Visualize yourself as highly magnanimous person. See yourself as strong, noble, just, caring, and helpful.

- Visualize having the finest intentions, a clear mind, and a good heart. See yourself as a person who others seek out. Picture living with great courage - you fear nothing because your heart is pure.

- Picture living modesty so that you always have more than you need, no matter what your income. Picture saving, building, and being charitable.

- Picture not seeking power and position, yet being so personally influential that power and position are given to you.

THE PHILOSOPHY OF TAOISM - AESTHETICS

LI (FORM OR ORGANIC PATTERN)

"Even on the road to hell flowers can make you smile."
– Deng Ming-Dao

DESCRIPTIONS:

The Chinese character *li* has several meanings including morality, correct behavior, inherent benevolence, and form. One of the most prominent philosophers in Chinese history, Chu His, considered *li* to be synonymous with the Tao.

Here we are viewing *li* in the sense of form. It is respect for the natural, informal, order of things. If there is a philosophic underpinning to *li*, it is that natural is beautiful.

Li literally means "markings in jade" or "grain in wood." This alludes to the nonsymmetrical order found everywhere in the natural world: the fiber of muscle, the asymmetrical designs in plants, the rough elegance of stones, the unique character of the landscape, or the water-carved sculptures of a riverbank.

***Li* is the organic order; the design of nature.**

To Taoists, *li* is an appreciation for the way things are naturally. It is not egocentrically assuming we know better than nature does. It means not second guessing the wisdom of biology. It means not arrogantly changing Earth's creations to conform to some man made conception.

Taoists respect, appreciate, and honor the animals, plants, and even rocks, ravines, and rivers for just as they are. They do not need to justify or find reasons for this. Why spoil the mysterious, subtle beauty of nature's art by analyzing it? (We could say the same of love.) Therefore, as Tao is the course, *li* is the watercourse – the natural flow of nature's design.

PRESCRIPTIONS:

If you rigidly hold on to concepts of beauty, begin to widen your vistas. It you are the type of person who needs things to be symmetrical, expand your appreciation for the artful character of the asymmetrical.

Do not make the mistake of continually imposing your aesthetic concepts on nature. Do not automatically assume that you must somehow *fix* the natural world to conform to a man made aesthetic conception. One example of *li* is in landscaping. Instead of a chemically drenched, labor-intensive, putting green, lawn, consider a natural landscape with indigenous, low-maintenance plants.

Learn to appreciate the course of Tao, and the watercourse of *li*. Relax and go with the natural design and flow of things. You will find that there is not really a good reason to hang on to your former restrictive views. Everything is beautiful in its own way. That does not mean that it has to be your style. Just let it be.

(From the West: *"In all things of nature there is something of the marvelous."* – Aristotle)

THE PHILOSOPHY OF TAOISM – METAPHYSICS

INTRODUCTION

"All the fish needs is to get lost in the water. All that man needs is to get lost in Tao." – Chuang Tzu

DEPARTURE:

Prepare yourself. In this part of *Taoism*, we venture into deep, dark, metaphysical waters. First, we will overview our planned course across the great sea of Taoist cosmology. Then we will set sail and explore each world along the way.

Note: During my research into the cosmology of the Tao, I searched for a concise summary of the "Story of All" - "The Big Bang of Taoism." I was after a step-by-step listing of the significant events that sequentially created everything. I did not find this expository themata of enigmatic cosmic elements. This does not mean that one does not exist somewhere. I just didn't find it. So what follows is my own conception based on my research. I stand ready to correct any misconceptions the reader may submit.

Classical Taoist teachings on cosmology are fragmented, and diverse in both style and content. Here, I have attempted to connect the most important events in time space into a logical sequence. Below is what I believe to be the top down chronological development of the mega events. It is a 10-point progressive schematization or cognitive framework for

Taoist metaphysics. The first, the Tao, was described in the "Introduction to Taoism." A brief description of the other structural elements follows.

TAOIST COSMOLOGY

1. The Tao is the eternal, infinite, <u>intelligence</u> and <u>power</u> that created, governs, and animates the world and universe.

2. From the Tao came c*h'ang* - the eternal, universal, unchanging laws that describe and determine the behavior of all things.

3. From the Tao came the virtue energy of *Te*, which gives all things the qualities that make them what they are - their fundamental natures.

4. From the Tao came the primordial beginning of *T'ai* or *T'ai-Chi* (the "Supreme One") from which all things arise with the energy of *chi*.

5. From *T'ai-Chi* came *yin* and *yang*.

6. *Yang-chi* ascended to become Heaven. *Yin-chi* descended to become Earth.

7. From the interaction of *yin* and *yang* (the movement of the Tao) came *I* (change or transformation).

8. From *I* came the five elements of earth, wood, fire, metal, and water.

9. From the five elements came *Wan-Wu* (the 10,000 things or literally everything).

10. In accord with *Fu* (reversal and return), *yin* and *yang* reverses to return to each other, and *Wan-Wu* returns to the Tao and *Wu* (non-being).

(From the West: *"The universe is like a safe to which there is a combination, but the combination is locked up in the safe."* – Peter de Vries)

CH'ANG (LAWS)

"The Tao abides in non-action, yet nothing is left undone." – Chapter 37 of the *Tao Te Ching*

DESCRIPTIONS:

INTRODUCTION:

From the Tao came c*h'ang* - the eternal, universal, unchanging laws that describe and determine the behavior of all things.

Science is what we "know". Philosophy is what we speculate. Both are attempts at understanding *ch'ang*.

Scientists hypothesize, experiment, observe, measure, induce, deduce, and formulate the behavior of phenomena. However, science remains silent about the more vexing questions of life such as those concerning values and ultimate reality. That which is not yet subject to scientific methods we speculate upon and call philosophy. Our science and philosophy are our attempts to understand the world, the universe, and ourselves.

In Taoist terms, all of this is *ch'ang* that we are attempting to understand. That is the unchanging, eternal, universal, laws of reality that underpin the nature of all things.

***Ch'ang* is the intelligence of the Tao at work.**

PERMANENCE AMID IMPERMANENCE:

Impermanence:

Impermanence is a central theme in Taoism. (As it is in the Buddhist concept of *anicca*.) Impermanence is conveyed in the cliché "*Everything changes.*"

The Great Exception to Impermanence:

What so many teachers and texts seem to overlook is that there is one great exception to the statement that everything changes – truth.

Truth of History:

The truth doesn't change. If it did, it would not be the truth. Reality is what it is at any point in the history of time and space. The fact that conditions change as time and space does, does not alter the truth of what reality *was*. It is forever a truth of history.

Truth of Laws:

Further, there are invisible laws creating and animating reality that also do not change. Within the context of Newtonian mechanics (i.e., not in the context of realms such as quantum physics), force equals mass times acceleration ($F = m \times a$). Under these conditions, force always has equaled mass times acceleration and always will. This permanence amid impermanence holds as well for all other laws.

Philosophic Taoism recognizes this great exception to impermanence (truth) in the concept of *ch'ang*. The laws of the universe are unchanging. *Ch'ang* is not conditional. It is not affected by temporal or spatial realities. Think of *ch'ang* as something you can *always* count on.

CH'ANG AND WU-WEI:

The entire idea of *wu-wei* (see "The Philosophy of Taoism – Ethics") is to let *ch'ang* do its work. Essentially *wu-wei* means the non-interference and cooperation with *ch'ang*.

PRESCRIPTIONS:

LEARN HISTORY:

Who is wise enough to study what has happened in order to better understand what is and what will be? Today is conditioned by a billion yesterdays. Tomorrow will be conditioned by today. Study history and you will better understand not only where you have been and where you are, but also where you are going.

LEARN THE LAWS:

Become an indefatigable analyst of human nature and natural phenomena. Be your own scientist. Observe, theorize, test, and confirm the works of everything important in your life. Search for and discover *ch'ang*.

OBEY THE LAWS:

Have respect for natural law. Learn to live in accordance with the eternal laws of *ch'ang*. Once mastered, practice entering *flow*, that natural and exhilarating state of optimal being where everything seems to go right.

TE (VIRTUE ENERGY)

DESCRIPTIONS:

TE:

From the intelligence and power of the Tao came the virtue energy of *te*, which gives all things the qualities that make them what they are i.e., their fundamental natures.

At the individual level, *te* brings the science and art of correct living. People with high *te* arrive at it, and express it naturally, without vanity, or artifice. High *te* individuals are characterized by the following virtues: intelligence, wisdom, creativity, self-control, personal responsibility, honesty, integrity, dignity, compassion, charity, patience, justice, and magnanimity.

TE AND *CHI:*

An introduction to *te* can lead one to believe that it is synonymous with *chi*. Both are referred to in Taoist literature as powers that endow all things with energy. But *te* is a special manifestation of *chi*. It is the power that creates, develops, and sustains the individual virtues of a thing that make it what it fundamentally is, and endows it with its appearance.

Te can be conceptualized as personalized *chi*.

VIRTUE IN TAOISM AND CONFUCIANISM:

Taoism departs from Confucianism in the origin of *te*. In Taoism *te* virtues evolve from the Tao. Confucian virtues evolve from societal norms.

PRESCRIPTIONS:

BELIEVE IN YOUR *TE*:

Begin today to recognize and believe in your personal manifestation of te. Everyone has virtues, even those farthest from the good path. There is an essential purity in everyone. The problem is that we bury it beneath a lifetime of soil.

LOOK INWARD:

Use your right-brain intuitive abilities to probe the depths of your being. Gain a sense of the nature of your personal te. Reflect what virtues you believe you possess and/or could cultivate. Find a quiet place where you can be still. Meditate. Look inward and find your personal spiritual best. Identify and even write down those that are core to your character.

CULTIVATE YOUR *TE*:

Use your intuitive powers to learn what increases your virtuous energy. Take note of the conditions under which you seem to soar to new spiritual heights. Test and refine them. Make the development of te a lifelong process.

RECOGNIZE AND ENCOURAGE THE *TE* IN OTHERS:

Look for the hidden virtues in others. See people not only as they are, but also as they could be. Consider how they would be if they were fully spiritually actualized. Treat them as if they were. Help them see what they are and can be. There is no greater gift you can ever give a person. We all want to be relevant, important, and respected by others.

CHI OR *QI* (COSMIC ENERGY)

"Before Heaven and Earth were separate, there was only the indefinable ONE. This ONE was divided and yin and yang came into existence. That which received yang-chi rose up bright and clear and became Heaven; that which received yin-chi sank down heavy and obscure and became Earth; and that which received both yin-chi and yang-chi in right proportions became man." – From the Taoist text *The Experience of the Golden Flower*

DESCRIPTIONS:

INTRODUCTION:

Chi or Qi:

The mysterious Tao - the ultimate source of all things – empowers all with *chi* (old name) *or qi* (new name). In Chinese, *chi* or *qi*; in Japanese *ki*, is pronounced "chee." It is similar to the concepts of *prana* in Hinduism, and
spiritus in Christianity. In homeopathic medicine, it is the *vital force* within the body. *Chi* is sometimes written as *ch'i*.

Chi is the energy from the Tao that animates all things.

Taoists refer to *chi* as the life force, *life breath,* or the *dragon's breath*. *Chi* is in all things both animate and inanimate.

Shen-Chi and Sha-Chi:

Shen-chi or *Sheng-chi* is supportive and empowering. It is conducive to wisdom, health, happiness, good fortune, and relationships.

Sha-chi is unsupportive and disempowering. It makes it harder for us to gain knowledge, maintain health, achieve peace of mind, become financially secure, and to achieve loving relationships.

Below is a table that provides a further description of the characteristics associated with *shen-chi* and *sha-chi*.

Shen-Chi	*Sha-Chi*
Positive	Negative
Balanced	Imbalanced
Harmonious	Disrupting
Orderly	Disorderly
Aesthetic	Unattractive
Balanced lighting	Too bright or too dark
Nature's sounds	Disturbing noises
Pleasant smells	Offensive odors
Healthy, satisfying tastes	Unhealthy, offensive tastes
Clean	Dirty
Healthy	Unhealthy
Comfortable	Uncomfortable
Calming	Irritating
Smooth soothing surfaces	Rough, risky, ragged
Gently curving flow	Abrupt straight flow
Spacious	Cluttered
Secure and safe	Insecure and unsafe
Any other pleasant sights, smells, sounds, and sensations.	Any other unpleasant sights, smells, sounds, and sensations.

Much of *Feng Shui* (See "*Feng Shui*" under the metaphysics) is about maximizing *shen-chi* and minimizing *sha-chi*.

Matter and Energy:

Taoists do not make a sharp distinction between matter and energy. Interestingly enough, modern physicists do not either. So *chi* can be conceived as manifesting in both forms. At the subatomic level, matter is patterns of energy. Some modern scientist-philosophers have interpreted *chi* as electromagnetic and kinetic energy.

> Note: In the metaphysical realm, many believe that old buildings retain a "memory" of happy, sad, or tragic events. Could it be that what people sense - especially that "eerie" feeling in certain places - is part of the "vibrating history" of *chi*?

MANIFESTATIONS:

<u>*Chi* on Earth:</u>

Chi is most obvious in the physical things on Earth – the land, terrain, water bodies, etc. They all vibrate at specific frequencies.

Chi manifests on Earth in a *yin* or passive state in protective geological features such as hills and mountains. It manifests in a *yang* or active state in the flow of wind and water.

<u>*Chi* in Us:</u>

Chi, like blood, continually flows through our body. Naturopaths have worked with this flow since antiquity. Homeopaths work to restore and maintain the "vital force." Eastern healers believe there to be seven *chokras* and 14 meridians conducting the flow of *chi* in the body. Acupuncture is now recognized as a legitimate treatment in the personal "free *chi*" movement. The health of our *chi* is a function of several factors including our thoughts, food, and external human and man-made environment.

A metaphor from physics and electrical engineering

might be useful to better understand how each of us relates to *chi*. We are like an extremely complex, intelligently designed microchip. When power (*chi*) is applied, the most efficient microchips (people) reliably perform their functions (our internal and external activities) according to their design (DNA, physiology, intentions, etc.). There is a minimum of energy-wasting, heat-producing, internal resistance (stress, conflicts, fatigue, etc.). Unimpeded current flows where there is harmony within the system (harmony with the Tao.)

Chi Above:

Chi is much less obvious in its invisible form. It is like frequencies of the electromagnetic spectrum that we cannot detect without instruments. This abstract form of *chi* is related to time, space, and directions. *Chi* energy travels in invisible lines from above.

Examples of *chi* above include the very real forces exhibited by the sun, the moon, the weather, and the variety of rays and particles that continually strike us with fantastic speeds.

TAOISM AND *CHI*:

Taoist spirituality is more than a sublime understanding or a peaceful state. It is a holistic expression of the natural self. It is also a virtuous, productive way of living in harmony with the flow of *chi*. This means rigorously removing and astutely avoiding the blockage and stagnation of *chi*.

Taoists take inventory of any impediments they may have to their connection with the Tao, and assiduously remove them. They naturally avoid those vain, futile, and complex enmeshments in life (back to simplicity again) that impede the free movement of *chi*. Taoists also avoid excessive concentrations of *chi*.

Balance in the *yin-yang* cycle is all.

The Taoist conception of *chi* force and the afterlife parallels many of the religions traditions in the West. They believe our physical form (matter) that gives us our appearance is impermanent. Our non-physical form (energy) that gives us our vitality survives death. Not too much should be read into this. The Taoist vision of the afterlife does not include a paradise where angels on clouds play harps.

FLOWING WITH *CHI*:

Here are just four ways *chi* is recognized and managed around the world:

- For centuries the Chinese have used acupuncture to manage pain and treat illnesses. They do this by unblocking stagnated energy channels, and by increasing the circulation of *chi* along the meridians of the body.

- Martial artists concentrate *chi* when they perform extraordinary physical feats such as breaking a stack of blocks with their bare hands.

- Many Asians, and now people around the world in many different cultures, practice *Tai Chi* to enhance their mental, physical, and emotional well-being.

- *Feng Shui* has been used for centuries, as it still is today, to design interiors and structures. The intent, outlined in a forthcoming section, is to enhance the gentle movement of *chi.*

IN THE WEST:

In the West, *chi* has an identify crises. It isn't even on the radar screen. This is largely because it has not been identified and measured in that showcase of lifeless things – the laboratory. Western philosophy has ignored it as well. Therefore, at the time of this writing, it remains largely unknown.

That said, at the subatomic level, western physicists have been observing energy patterns that are surprisingly like the ancient concept of *chi*.

Perhaps one day the different east-west approaches to this phenomenon will converge in a mutual understanding as they have done in so many others concepts.

PRESCRIPTIONS:

TUNE IN:

First, develop a sense and appreciation for your personal *chi*. Notice your different *chi* energy states: when it surges; when it flows free and strong; and when it becomes stagnant and blocked. You will especially notice a blockage when you are suffering from a hole in our heart, perhaps due to the loss of a loved one. This awareness requires that you are "in your body" - that you are present and in tune with it.

HEAL:

Are you leaking energy? Are you hemorrhaging your life force? Do you find yourself obsessed with a past wrong? Do you fight off the demons that arise in your mind? Do you find yourself shadow boxing a ghost from your past? Are you in the justification or rationalization process to settle an old issue? Do you engage in mental polemics with those who are not there? Are you spewing out to others in a desperate attempt to gain agreement?

If so, you must make healing your top priority. We are talking here about those experiences in life that leave a tear in your soul. They could originate from neglect, abuse, or betrayal. There are also those that are self-inflicted. You could be aware of them, or in denial about them. Signs of these afflictions include a troubled mind, insomnia, lack of appetite, sickness, and simply a heavy heart.

The principles and practices of Taoism, Buddhism, and Zenism hold the secrets to healing. Study and use them in your healing process.

UNBLOCK YOUR *CHI*:

Start by removing any lumpy blockages you may have to the flow of you personal *chi*. (Your personal "free-*chi* movement.") Try *T'ai Chi* or *Qigong* to improve the current of *chi* through your body. If you need help, consider using the services of a qualified acupuncturist or kinesiologist to balance your internal *Feng Shui*.

Systematically eliminate everything that is toxic in your life. This includes all toxic thoughts, food, drink, entertainment, people, jobs, possessions, and environments. End all those activities, which block, drain, or otherwise dissipate or weaken your life-giving *chi*.

ENHANCE YOUR *CHI*:

Enhance the vitality and movement of *chi* within you. Purify your intentions. Maintain a bright, strong, positive outlook on life. Visualize yourself as a person with a very high level of life force that is directed to the greatest good. Engage in those activities in your life which release and replenish your *chi*. Feel more alive, and live to the fullest.

(From the West: *Aristotle was right: there is a power*

within that molds every form, in plants and planets, in animals and men. – Schopenhauer)

YIN AND *YANG* (POLARITY)

"The Tao begot one. One begot two. Two begot three. And three begot the ten thousand things. The ten thousand things carry yin and embrace yang. They achieve harmony by combining these forces." – Chapter 42 of the *Tao Te Ching*

DESCRIPTION:

INTRODUCTION:

***Yin* and *yang* are the two dynamic and polar forces of the Tao that continually interact to create all things.**

MISUNDERSTANDINGS:

First we must clear up a few misunderstandings about the concept of *yin-yang*:

Not Independent:

Yin and *yang* are a dimorphic semi-fiction. There is no such thing as *pure yin* or *pure yang*. They are always intertwined (*hsiang sheng*). Within *yang*, there is always some *yin*; within *yin*, there is always some *yang*. They are forever bonded together in mutual dependency as cosmic Siamese twins. The one cannot be defined, or even exist, without the other. (Like men and women.)

Not Female or Male:

Yin and *yang* are not gender related. They are not female and male. However out of convenience, the adjectives "feminine" and "masculine" are used to describe the qualities of the two.

Not Advantageous or Disadvantageous:

Neither *yin* nor *yang* should be described as "good" or "bad." They are both morally and practically neutral. We need each. However, an imbalance in either can bring difficulties.

Not Absolute:

Everything is relative. Anything (an object, a wall, a hillside) can be *yin* when their surroundings are *yang*, and *yang* when their surroundings are *yin*. While the moon is listed in the table that follows as *yin* relative to the sun, it could be *yang* relative to the night sky.

IN THE EAST:

We will first review the Eastern Taoist concept of *yin-yang*. We will then we will explore the Western analog.

COSMOLOGY:

To repeat a portion of the earlier summary of Taoist cosmology:

- **From the Tao came the cosmic energy of *Chi* with the primordial beginning of *T'ai* or *T'ai-Chi* (the "Supreme One") from which all things arise.**

- **From *T'ai-Chi* came *yin* and *yang*.**

- ***Yang-chi* ascended to become Heaven. *Yin-chi* descended to become Earth.**

- **From the interaction of *yin* and *yang* (the movement of the Tao) came *I* (change or transformation).**

SYMBOLS:

The symbol for *yin* is a broken line (_ _), referred to as a negative line. The symbol for *yang* is a single solid line (_), referred to as positive line.

QUALITIES:

Originally, *yin* meant the dark side of the mountain and the north shore of the river. *Yang* meant the light side of the mountain and the south shore of the river. *Yin* also mean "No", and *yang* "Yes." Over time, the polar concepts of *yin* and *yang* evolved to mean much more. The below tables illustrate how these two opposing forces are on opposite ends of a number of continuums:

Yin	*Yang*
Feminine	Masculine
Downward	Upward
Inward	Outward
Sleep	Wake
Passive or static	Active or dynamic
Pacifistic	Combative
Decay	Growth
Death	Life
Soft	Hard
Low	High
Interior	Exterior
Garden	House
Still water	Streams
Valleys	Hills and mountains
Winter	Summer
Cold	Warm
Dark	Light
Moon	Sun
Earth	Heaven
Water	Fire
Even numbers	Odd numbers

CYCLES:

Yin and *yang* do their creative dance to the music of the Tao. Each ebbs and flows in a systole and diastole of ascendancy and decadency. In the cycles of *yin* and *yang*, we see *the principle of the leveling of opposites*. One takes the lead and rises to dominance only to peak, decline, and relinquish lead to the other in an endless exchange through time and space.

We see the counterbalanced duality of *yin* and *yang* on a grand scale in nature. In the daily cycle, we are active (*yang*) during the light (*yang*) of day, and rest (*yin*) during the dark (*yin*) of night. There are the cycles of the sun and the moon, and the seasons. We even find the dynamic tension of *yin-yang* at the subatomic level with positive proton and negative electron. What would our reality be without this fundamental *yin-yang* polarity? Would there even be a reality?

FU:

This is an appropriate time to refer to the concept of *Fu*. *Yin* and *yang* continually demonstrate a return or reversion to their opposite. This is an example of the Taoist concept of *Fu* or return. (See "*Fu*" later in the section on metaphysics.)

BALANCE:

The cycles of *yin* and *yang* seem to continually interact around an axis of situational balance in coherence with the Tao. There are many analogs: In the human body, there is the tendency toward homeostasis. In statistics, there are the measures of central tendency (*mean, median, mode*). In Western thought there is Aristotle's Golden Mean. In Eastern thought there is Buddha's Middle Way.

IN THE WEST

We will now review the Western analog of *yin-yang*. The concept of *yin-yang* duality is not foreign to Western thinkers. It has counterparts in the *Eternal Cycles*, *Eternal Reoccurrence*, and *The Doctrine of Universal Reversion*. What follows are what I believe to be two examples of how the concept of *yin-yang* has influenced Western thinkers. The first is from the field of philosophy. The second is from the field of psychology.

PHILOSOPHY:

Introduction:

Baruch Spinoza, a.k.a. Benedictus De Spinoza, (1632 – 1677) developed a concise philosophical system. Within it, among many other great thoughts, he provided a solution to the moral dilemma that has faced many: to be strong and warlike, or to be accommodating and peaceful. (Beware here of the "binary trap.")

This quandary seems to especially plague males in the course of their development. On one hand, they are socially conditioned to be strong, independent warriors. (Developmentalists refer to this identification as "self-in-isolation.") On the other hand, we are chided for not being sensitive, compassionate, and relational. (The identification of "self-in-relation.") Spinoza reconciled these two polar ethical systems into one harmonious unity (the *yin-yang* ideal).

Ethical System-1:

This is the feminine (*yin*) position. (Not to be confused with gender.) It is passive, inward, peaceful, and humanitarian. *Good* is equated with love and compassion, and manifests with unselfish service to the weak and suffering. All people are equally valuable, and all people should have equal rights - regardless of their limitations. Jesus Christ personified this ethic. Societies with this belief tend toward a pure form of communism and socialism.

Ethical System-2:

This is the masculine (*yang*) position. It is active, outward, dominating, and dispassionate. *Good* is equated with strength and power. It exerts itself with competition, confrontation, and domination. People are naturally unequal. It is absurd to try to make everyone the same. Might makes right. Machiavelli and Nietzsche personify its ethics and morality. Societies with this belief tend toward aristocracies of ability (not blood), and strong man dictatorships.

Analysis:

How do we analyze these extremes? Each has pros and cons. The first soft position has a laudable heart, but would never survive as the fittest in the deadly competition of the Darwinian world. To quote one sage: "*Make yourself a lamb, and the wolves will eat you.*"

The second strong position has a compelling argument: Who does not want to be strong? Who can make a virtue of weakness? But there is something in human nature that unfailingly reaches out to help the weak, the oppressed, and even our defeated enemy.

Reconciliation - Ethical System-3:

Spinoza brilliantly resolves this dilemma of having to choose between these two extremes. Ethically, it is a blend of the above two political systems. He follows in the tradition of Buddha and Aristotle by taking the *middle path* or *Golden Mean*.

This third ethical system is the ideal synergy between *yin* and *yang*. *Good* is equated with intelligence, knowledge and wise judgment. It is informed, wise, capable, flexible, balanced, and appropriate to the situation. There is a time when *yin* should dominate, and a time when *yang* should dominate.

When appropriate to the situation, this way is passive (remember *wu-wei*), compassionate, helpful, friendly, and even loving. But this does not mean that it is seeks peace at any price. There are times when diplomacy fails, and a peaceful solution is impossible. The choices are fight or die. This calls for intelligence, strength, and courage. It calls for the last resort - war like action. There are situations under which pacifism is simply wrong.

There are even conditions under which life is not worth living.

PSYCHOLOGY:

Introduction:

Dr. Carl Gustav Jung (1875 – 1961) proposed that, in the human psyche, the male and female both had characateristics of the other. This "gender residue" is similar to the way *yang* always manifests with elements of *yin*, and *yin* always manifests with elements of *yang*. (Hence the dot of each in the other in the *yin-yang* symbol on the cover of this book.)

Anima and Animus:

Jung wrote that the male (*yang*) psyche harbors subconscious feminine (*yin*) psychological tendencies personified in what he called the *anima*. A man's mother strongly conditions his *anima*, which often emerges in fantasies.

In turn, the female (*yin*) psyche harbors subconscious masculine (*yang*) psychological tendencies personified in what Jung called the *animus*. A woman's father conditions her *animus*, which often appears in her strong convictions.

We can gain some idea of our *anima* and *animus* by studying our dreams. The proper role of each is to reconcile differences between ego (conscious personality) and self (totality of psyche).

Subconscious:

Jung's conception of *anima* and *animus* (along with others) takes place in the *sub*conscious level, so we may not be aware of it at all. Further, the subconscious is a vast realm that dwarfs the conscious.

As Jung describes it:

"*The conscious mind moreover is characterized by a certain narrowness. It can only hold a few simultaneous contents at a given moment. All the rest is unconscious at the time, and we only get a sort of continuation or a general understanding or awareness of a conscious world through the succession of conscious moments. We can never hold an image of totality because our consciousness is too narrow.... The area of the unconscious is enormous and always continuous, while the area of the consciousness is a restricted field of momentary vision.*"

Biological Origins:

One could speculate that these psychological constructs of Jung derive from our biological dimorphism (two different forms in the same specie) i.e., we have the potential to be either sex.

Each human *gamete* (sperm and ovum) holds more than a billion chemical codes or genetic instructions.
In the first hour or so after the sperm and ovum combine, they retain their separate identities. Then they suddenly join to form a living cell called a *zygote*. Soon growth begins through division and duplication.

All human embryos begin as females.

If the y-chromosome is present, at about the sixth week of gestation male differentiation begins. If it is not present, the default gender is female.

If all of us men could just remember our common female origins, perhaps through this affiliation, we would be less inclined to mistreat our gender counterparts.

SOME LAST WORDS ON *YIN, YANG*, AND GENDER:

Yin has been associated with women, *yang* with men. However, as described above in the theories of Carl Jung, each gender contains traces of the other.

At first it seems, especially from our modern experience, that men and women are doomed to endless gender wars, and ceaseless struggles for supremacy. The militant extremists in both camps fan the flames of combat, and even hatred.

But the thinking man or woman sees beyond the provinciality of his or her gender, and realizes that this competitive model is very limited. They know that we can live much happier and fuller lives through mutual understanding, respect, and cooperation than we ever could on the warpath.

The great hidden message, often neglected in Taoist literature on *yin-yang* is this: gender differences offer us endless possibilities for cooperation and creativity among men and women. The equally great *yin-yang* forces continually interplay to create a dynamic synthesis. The whole is greater than the sum of its parts.

Women and men need each other to not only complete themselves, but to create something very beautiful and wonderful *beyond* themselves.

The great social challenge for men and women everywhere is to recognize, honor, and harmonize their unique *yin-yang* voices into a sweet symphony of love and life. (A predictable thought from a quintessentially romantic Libra author.)

PRESCRIPTIONS:

STOP THE GENDER WAR:

Despite the opportunities for hostilities that are so pervasive in Western culture, refuse to bash the opposite sex. Replace the destructive *us against them* social view, with one of intelligent cooperation.

Yin and *yang* forces necessarily exist in all of us. One is as important as the other. They exist to harmonize with each other, not to wage war. If you are struggling with any internal or external gender wars, cease-fire, end destructive thoughts, seek understanding, and gain inner peace (See "Inner Peace" in "The Psychology of Taoism.")

Rise above gender bickering. Do your part to end the battles. Be honest, objective, and just, no matter what the gender of the disputant. Be mindful of double standards. Reconcile them up, not down. Fashion yourself into the apotheosis of the magnanimous gentleman or gentlewoman that you could be.

LET GO OF PAST HURTS:

The cessation of hostilities between genders may be particularly difficult if you have been mistreated, abused, or betrayed. If this is your case, know that letting go of past hurts is one of the greatest gifts you can ever give yourself.

Letting go doesn't mean that a wrong that was done to you is no longer wrong. It also doesn't mean that you should forget the lesson learned. As the saying goes: "*Fool me once, shame on you. Fool me twice, shame on me.*"

Letting go does mean that you will no longer let the past cripple your capacity to be happy in the future.

RECOGNIZE AND VALUE *YIN-YANG* ELEMENTS:

Remember that *yin* and *yang* forces are both essential to progress and to being a balanced and effective human being. Use the fact that their complimentarity is synergistically creative. Recognize the dynamic interplay of the opposing forces of *yin* and *yang* within you. Value both as essential, creative forces in your life. Do not make the mistake of denying or undervaluing either. Do not let vanity or *machismo* hijack the development of your character and spiritual progress.

To effectively use both *yin* and *yang* forces within you, you must learn to effectively deal with conflict. Because of the constant movement and cyclical nature of existence, there are bound to be differences that arise from the rate and direction of change. Learn to view the tensions and even conflicts that inevitably arise as opportunities for learning and growth. Become skillful at situational jujitsu – turning potentially injurious conflicts into deeper levels of understanding.

INTELLIGENTLY APPLY *YIN* AND *YANG*:

Einstein said: "*Make things as simple as possible, but no simpler.*" In an attempt to simplify things, many people make the mistake of always using one approach to situations. Some always lead with their hearts, others with their minds, and still others with their force. Do not fall into the trap of *always* assuming one posture with people and with the world.

For *both men and women*, there is a time to be passive, yielding, and submissive (*yin*), and there is a time to be active, assertive, and resistant (*yang*). There is a time to be soft, understanding, and compassionate (*yin*), and a time to be firm, unyielding, and even combative (*yang*).

Be versatile in the use of your intelligence to know which is which. Where the situation requires weighing the pros and cons of known data in a linear, logical, deliberative manner, employ your rationalistic, analytical, left brain. Where the situation requires piercing through the unmanageably complex, the little known, or the unknown, employ your intuitive, holistic right-brain. Knowing when to use each requires great awareness, sensitivity, insight, flexibility, and self-discipline.

Go outward when there is a need for self-expression or leadership. Take action when it is proper and advantageous to do so. Know when you must fight for a worthy cause. Be strong and courageous when facing evil. Know that there are some circumstances so extreme that your life is worth risking.

At the same time, have the sense to know when to respond to truculence with understanding; to recalcitrance with patience; to suffering with loving kindness.

Modulate the high and low voltage of your personality to be fitting to the changing situations of your life.

(From the West: "*Nothing is so strong as gentleness and nothing is so gentle as real strength.*" - Ralph W. Sockman)

I (CHANGE)

"*The most wise and the most stupid do not change.*" - Confucius

DESCRIPTIONS:

TRANSLATION:

***I* (as in the *I Ching*) means "change" or "transformation."**

It is an important and ubiquitous idea in the philosophy of Taoism, and therefore warrants a separate but brief mention here.

I AND *YIN-YANG*:

The Tao flows with the dynamic interplay of *yin* and *yang*. As they confoundingly dissolve into each other, *change (I)* occurs.

MORALITY:

To be in harmony with *I,* is to respond to situations with the highest of moral intent – especially for duty beyond ones self.

NATURAL ADAPTATION:

According to Chaung Tzu, the *shen-jen* ("spiritual man" or "ideal man") becomes one with the Tao, and therefore no longer needs to be methodical i.e., he naturally and instinctively adapts to change, and thereby becomes liberated from the anxieties and problems of it.

STAGES OF PROGRESS:

As she goes through life, the Taoist recognizes the need for change, and doesn't resist it. She thoroughly completes each stage in her spiritual progress. When the time comes, and not before or after, she easily matriculates with ease and grace to the next stage of her development.

PRESCRIPTIONS:

RECOGNIZE THE TWO PATHS OF CHANGE:

Recognize that there are essentially two paths of change: all that is happening outside of you, and all that is happening inside of you.

While all the things going on outside of you may be interesting, your inner journey is most important to you. While you may live in the outer world, you can only experience it through your inner world.

UNDERSTAND YOUR BASIC LIFE OPTIONS:

Understand and appreciate that, as you go through life, you do *not* have the option of staying the same. Realize that the world is continuously changing, and you are changing along with it. Therefore, you have the first of two basic life options: change for the better or change for the worse? The better change is toward the Tao. The worse is away from it.

Assuming that you choose to change for the better, you have two other basic life options: maximize your change for the better or not? Why not become all you can be in this life?

Tune in to the Tao. Be in a harmonic convergence with it. Transform for the best with it.

This requires the art and the science of living. Perfect both all through your life.

WU-HSING (THE FIVE ELEMENTS)

DESCRIPTIONS:

INTRODUCTION:

To position ourselves on our journey though our exploration of Taoist cosmology, let's review:

From the movement of the Tao came the interaction of *yin* and *yang*. From the interaction of *yin* and *yang* came *I* (change or transformation). From *I* came the five elements of earth, wood, fire, metal, and water.

The Chinese believe that the dynamic interplay of *yin* and *yang* produce these five elements from which all else evolves.

Wu-Hsing (*Wu-Te*, "The Five Virtues", "The Five Energies", "The Five Movers", "The Five Phases of Transformation") is found throughout the principles and practices of Taoism.

CLARIFICATION:

"The Five Elements" should not be literally interpreted as the actual substances of earth, wood, fire, metal, and water. Rather they are symbols of the *qualities* of these substances.

For instance, water symbolizes a flowing, adaptive, yet powerful force, not water itself.

THE FIVE ELEMENTS TABLE:

The table below summarizes the *wu-hsing* elements; their associated *yin (even,* Earth, perfecting) *–yang* (odd, Heaven, originating) number, direction; color; taste, organs, emotion, symbolism; representative objects; the way they affect each other; and their positive and negative potentials. Note that wind – an element in some other traditions – is not included.

	Earth	**Wood**	**Fire**	**Metal**	**Water**
Yin-Yang No.	5,10	3,8	2,7	4,9	1,6
Place	center	east	south	west	north
Color	yellow	green	red	White silver gold	blue black
Taste	sweet	sour	bitter	sharp	salty
Organ	stomach pancreas muscles mouth	eyes liver gall bladder sinews	heart blood vessels small intestine tongue	large intestine lung nose hairs	kidneys bladder bones ears
Feeling	worry	anger	joy	sadness	fear
Season	mid summer	spring	summer	autumn	winter
Symbol	nurture fertile	growth yielding straight-tening	light heat rising	strength mallea-bility	Moisten-ing flexible flowing

Décor Objects	pottery	flowers plants	candles fireplace	any quality metal piece	fountain fish tank
Positive Effects	stable reliable loyal patient nurture use for solitude and healing	vision growing fun social	leader-like high energy use for debating energy innovation	Discipline focus organize independent, powerful use for wealth gain and success	Sensitive intuitive use to reflect, communicate learning convincing
Negative Effects	minutia-focused	edgy sensitive lack of follow through	edgy impulse unruly not sensitive exploiting	Inflexible stern	hyper-sensitive flip invasive
Increase by...	fire	water	wood	earth	metal
Reduce by...	wood	metal	water	fire	earth
Raises	metal	fire	earth	water	wood
Lowers	water	earth	metal	wood	fire

APPLICATIONS:

The Chinese have adopted The Five Elements to many diverse applications including organs of the body, *Feng Shui*, compass directions, colors, numbers, seasons of the year, and other systems.

PRESCRIPTIONS:

USE THE FIVE ELEMENTS IN *FENG SHUI*:

Refer to the discussion of The Five Elements in the following subject on *Feng Shui* to understand how to use the elements in a home or office.

USE THE FIVE ELEMENTS IN TCM:

Traditional Chinese Medicine (TCM) uses The Five Elements to describe various conditions of the body. A complete description of this discipline could fill several volumes.

Introduce yourself to TCM and you will discover a natural way to regain and maintain your physical health.

FENG SHUI (WIND AND WATER)

DESCRIPTIONS:

INTRODUCTION:

Feng translates to "wind", and *shui* to "water." (The wind transports and scatters *chi*, and the water stores it.)

Feng Shui (pronounced "Fung Shway") **is the ancient Chinese art and science of optimizing the flow of *Chi*.**

Feng Shui involves the study of invisible patterns of energy and how we interact with them.

WHY STUDY *FENG SHUI*?

Recall our study of *chi*:

***Chi* is the energy from the power of the Tao that animates all things.**

Taoists refer to *chi* as the life force, *life breath* or the *dragon's breath.*

Everything keeps moving and changing in this mysterious universe. We can make our life more successful if we work with, and not against, the energy behind the flux of this change. The key in this process, and a central tenant of *Feng Shui* is to maintain a proper *yin-yang* balance in all things.

TAOISM AND *FENG SHUI*:

Remember that Taoism is about harmony with nature in general, and *chi* and *yin-yang* in particular.

***Feng Shui* is that instrumentality of Taoism that seeks harmony through the intelligent inclusion and placement of man-made objects and structures.**

Feng Shui is not only compatible with Taoism, Buddhism, and Zenism but is also compatible with *any* belief system that recognizes the wisdom of working with, rather than against, natural forces.

GEOMANCY:

Some consider *Feng Shui* to be a form of *geomancy*, and the term is often associated with it. The word *geomancy* derives from two ancient Greek words. *Geo* is from *Gaia* meaning the *Goddess of the Earth*. *Mancy* is from *manteia,* meaning divination. *Geomancy* studies soil patterns, terrain, watercourses and other geological features to enhance the prospects of happiness and prosperity.

THEORY AND PRACTICE DIFFERENCES:

We should remember the following three differences as

we begin to explore the mysterious and fascinating subject of *Feng Shui*:

Evolutionary Differences:

As the art and science of *Feng Shui* progressed, it experienced the differentiation that so typifies the evolution of complex systems. Differences in theories, led to differences in practices, and consequently differences in schools.

There are contemplative, magical, mystical, and divinational schools of *Feng Shui* - each with dedicated practitioners and well-established markets. So today an analysis of the same person, structure, or environment could yield some different conclusions depending on the perspective of the analyst.

For instance, one person might quickly arrive at an intuitive answer; another might derive a quite different one from a complex calculation using the *Lo P'an*. Trigrams are assigned fixed compass positions in one practice, but they change directions in another. It is easy to fall into the trap of picking a favorite perspective or approach, and then defending your position. I recommend avoiding impassioned debates over such subjective and provincial matters.

Keep in mind the fundamental purpose of *Feng Shui*: to optimize the flow of Ch'i.

Interpretation Differences:

Even within the same branch of *Feng Shui*, there are differing interpretations and practices. This diversity even extends to fundamentals. An example of this heterogeneity is the different listings of the four directions in the East-West dichotomy determined by the "Magic Number."

Individual Differences:

Perceptions of the same situation, even between people in the same family, can vary greatly. There is a great subjectivity to the interpretation of all the different applications of *yin* and *yang*.

For example, one person will think a room is far too dark (too *yin*). Another person will think is far too bright (too *yang*) - especially someone who is light sensitive or prone to migraines.

THE MULTIFACTORIAL NATURE OF FORTUNE:

In our study of *Feng Shui*, we should keep in mind that our well being, happiness, and prosperity are a function of *many* factors. The Chinese believe that luck, destiny, virtue, and knowledge combine with *Feng Shui* to create the fortunes of our life. Chinese Buddhists also believe in the inexorable law of *karma*.

The point here is that, as helpful as *Feng Shui* may be, it is one factor among several that determines our destiny. It cannot and does not nullify the influence of other factors. So if a brilliant *Feng Shui* design does not seem to produce good fortune, do not abandon the practice. Study the situation for other powerful, oppositional forces at play.

FENG SHUI EXPERIENCES:

Introduction:

You may not be aware of it, but most likely you are already familiar with the effects of *Feng Shui*. If you have experienced either of the following situations, you now may have some idea of how your surroundings can affect you. An awareness of this cause and effect connection is key to understanding *Feng Shui*.

Positive *Feng Shui* Experiences:

Did you ever enter a home or building where you immediately felt a sense of peace? Were you ever in a forum with people were amicable and just seemed to flow well? Were you ever in a work setting where you consistently produced timely and good results?

If the answer was "Yes" to any of the above questions, then you were most likely in life-enhancing *Feng Shui* environments for you. You were surrounded by the free flow of positive *chi*, called *sheng* (generating) *qi*.

Negative *Feng Shui* Experiences:

Conversely, did you ever enter a place where you had a strange ill-at-ease feeling, as if you were at risk? Did you ever have a general inability to connect with people? Can you recall a situation where you seem to be struggling against a hidden handicap, and your efforts were unsuccessful?

If any of these experiences are familiar to you, you now know what a negative, burdensome, energy-draining *Feng Shui* condition is like.

Quick Test:

A way to quickly test the quality of the *Feng Shui* wherever you are is to ask yourself these two simple questions: "How do I feel?" and "How are things going for me?"

SKEPTICISM:

There is much skepticism in the West about the legitimacy of *Feng Shui*. For some it is difficult to believe that the arrangement of things affects thoughts, feelings, and outcomes. Doubters should recall that, not long ago, there was a lot of skepticism, and even ridicule, about several other Eastern practices that are now mainstream. Three examples are meditation, *Tai Chi*, and acupuncture.

TWO BASIC REASONS WHY *FENG SHUI* WORKS:

It may *not* be necessary for us to understand *why Feng Shui* works, only that it *does* work. Nevertheless, for the skeptical, Western reader who requires proof of efficacy, I offer two basic reasons why you can take *Feng Shui* seriously: It works for physical and for psychological reasons.

PHYSICAL REASONS:

Introduction:

ced*Feng Shui* works for physical reasons simply because our surroundings affect our efficiency and effectiveness.

We know from common experience that there are advantageous and disadvantageous conditions for everything we do. In some milieus, we feel secure and confident. In others we do not.

Environments with effective *Feng Shui* tangibly support our cognition, judgments, health, peace, motivation, physical movements, productivity, happiness, and relationships. Environments with ineffective *Feng Shui* do not support these dimensions of our life, and leave us vulnerable and insecure.

All That's Old Is New Again:

The practice of *Feng Shui* begins with character. It continues with the intelligent analysis of the purpose of a structure. Inner and outer elements are then located to optimize the intended results.

In modern architectural design and industrial engineering this sequential process is summarized in the principle that *form follows function*. Sometimes this functionality is apparent and measurable. Other times it is obscure and unquantifiable.

> Note: A fascinating research project would be to analyze physical layouts based on *Feng Shui* principles to determine how well they accord with the industrial engineering disciplines of *motion and time study*, and *methods analysis*.

Apparent Physical Reasons:

There are physical reasons why *Feng Shui* works that are quite apparent. We can easily see when a physical condition such as light, air, and structures assist our functionality.

If you are ever uneasy about your vulnerability when your back is to a door, then you can begin to understand the *Feng Shui* concept of the *Back Turtle*. This is the positioning of structures, hills, or mountains in back of, or to the north of you to protect against wind, cold, or attack.

Unapparent Physical Reasons:

There are physical reasons why *Feng Shui* works that are not apparent. Some are simply hidden. Others are below or above the perceptual thresholds of our sense organs.

Example: We are continually being bombarded by different frequencies of electromagnetic waves. We swim in a sea of invisible waves. Further, all the "solid" matter around us is really energy in motion. It is hard to believe, but everything is moving.

Even if we do not sense or understand these unapparent physical reasons why *Feng Shui* works, it seems reasonable that we should flow with, rather than struggle against, them.

PSYCHOLOGICAL REASONS:

Introduction:

Feng Shui works for psychological reasons. We will briefly cover three below: awareness, associations, and the self-fulfilling prophecy.

Awareness:

The first reason that *Feng Shui* works for psychological reasons is because, at some level, we are aware of the content and structure of our surroundings. The more congruent they are with our fundamental nature and goals, the more peaceful, focused, and successful we will be. Conversely, the less congruent the content and structure of our surroundings are with our fundamental nature and goals, the more unsettled, distracted, and challenged we will be. For example, it is not wise to have office work and business furniture in a bedroom. The work component is distracting when you are tying to fall to sleep.

Associations:

The second reason *Feng Shui* works for psychological reasons is because our environments contain objects that have both positive and negative associations for us. Some objects trigger superficial associative links. Others trigger deep, emotionally charged memories.

One example of such an object-association link is the *Feng Shui* concept of a *shar*. A *shar* is any line, edge, object, or structure inside or outside that appears (not usually is) threatening. Such elements as decorations, furniture, counters, walls, sidewalks, driveways, or roads can be *shars*. While we consciously know these are normal objects, we subconsciously interpret these protuberances as dangerous because their form is associated with piercing objects. In *Feng Shui*, these undesirable features are also called *hidden, secret,* or *poison arrows*. Some *shars* or poison arrows are easy to identify. If an object looks like a spear, it is understandable that we could subconsciously consider it a symbolic threat. However, other associations are much more complex, and deeply subliminal – below our level of conscious perception. So, we once again enter the world of Dr. Carl Jung. His research led him to his concept of *archetypes*. These are powerful, enduring, subconscious symbols common to the collective mind of human beings in every culture throughout history.

> Note: Perhaps someday, some inquisitive soul will test this question: Is there a correlation between the principles and practices of *Feng Shui* and the mystical influences of Jung's archetypes?

Self-Fulfilling Prophecy:

The third reason that *Feng Shui* works for psychological reasons relates to the *self-fulfilling prophecy*. To simply state this idea, what we believe to be true, we attract into our life. So if our surroundings mirror our values and goals, we are more likely to focus on them, and attract them into our life. Conversely, if our surroundings are antithetical to our values and goals, we are more likely to focus on, and attract the opposite.

As a positive example, if we expect that a room in our home or office will be propitious (a word often used in *Feng Shui*) for a certain activity, then we will consciously and subconsciously work to make that expectation come true.

As a negative example, an environment does not have to be obviously or strongly threatening to limit us. Subtle non-supportive elements in our surroundings can slowly and perniciously misguide us, drain our strength, erode our motivation and drag us down over time. Many people metaphorically describe their social or work situation as *"draining my will to live."*

A BRIEF HISTORY OF *FENG SHUI*:

Origins:

The origin of *Feng Shui* dates back to around 4000 B.C. *Feng Shui,* and perhaps even Taoism itself, evolved from an intuitive/empirical approach of practical experiment, observation, and analysis. The great legacy of *Feng Shui* and Taoist principles is the distilled result of countless trial-and-error, and trial-and-success experiments in thousands of settings over thousands of years.

Science and Art:

Feng Shui evolved as a science and an art. The science developed in conjunction with ancient Chinese philosophy, psychology, astrology, astronomy, mathematics, physics, interior design, architecture, agriculture, ecology, geography, geology, and meteorology. The art of *Feng Shui* developed from the intuition, creativity, skill, and *Kaizen*-esque refinement of its many practitioners. Superstition, folklore, and custom, also influenced its evolution.

Over many hundreds of years, the ancient Chinese kings, philosophers, shamans, and peasantry noticed what conditions were helpful to personal and economic success, and which were harmful. They began to record, share, and pass on their findings. Over time consistencies and patterns evolved. So the principles and practices of *Feng Shui* that emerged are not the result of superstition or guesswork. They are the result of a very long, objective, methodical, concise, and mostly rationalistic process.

The process and evolution of *Feng Shui* is not unlike that of folk medicine. Today, clinical studies are slowly confirming the efficacy of herbal, homeopathic, and other non-traditional cures that have been used for countless centuries by naturopaths.

At times, the guidelines and rules of *Feng Shui* may seem needlessly intricate, tedious, and even dispensable. But we might be more patient with them by remembering that they survived and evolved through many eras from countless experiments in a great diversity of settings. This gives them a credibility that we should respect.

Beginnings:

One of the earliest applications of *Feng Shui* occurred thousands of years ago when the first practitioners observed the locations of celestial bodies. They then aligned their sovereign's tombs with them. This practice slowly developed as a secret body of knowledge known only to a privileged few in the courts of Chinese emperors. Perhaps it was from these esoteric beginnings that *Feng Shui* began. It evolved in complexity and differentiated to fit the ever-changing and ever-widening man-made inclusions on the landscape of the Earth.

Today:

Today, millions of people around the world believe it is prudent - even essential - to faithfully adhere to the principles of *Feng Shui*. Many Chinese take great care to ensure the natural flow of *chi* in their homes with the proper arrangement of structures, furniture, and decorations.

Real estate developers and architects in the Orient routinely seek *xianshengs* or *geomancers* for advice in all stages of the design of grand projects. *Feng Shui* has been applied to structures ranging from skyscrapers in Hong Kong and the Disney Park, to great manufacturing plants around China. Investors and owners understand that the stakes are simply too great to risk being out of harmony with the universal forces of nature.

Feng Shui experts also advise on how to solve problems with existing structures to unblock the flow of *chi*, allow harmony to return, and bring good fortune to the enterprise. There are many stories of businesses that were on the brink of failure being saved by a propitious *Feng Shui* analysis and redesign.

Survival Value:

Time is the test of quality.

Any person, place, or thing can look and perform well in the early stages of life. But only that which has true, intrinsic quality looks and performs well over time.

There are never any guarantees, but the probability of something being reliable that has a long record of doing so is much better than that of the latest, untested fad. This is why the great historian Will Durant emphasized that in the adolescent anarchy of our youth, we should hesitate to diminish and destroy those traditions that have served so many, so well, for so long.

Westerners would be wise to recognize and respect the survival value of such a venerable tradition as *Feng Shui*. Whether you believe in it or not, the fact is that millions of people have practiced *Feng Shui* in different parts of the world for perhaps 6000 years. Its great cross-cultural appeal allowed it to spread through every aspect of Chinese society, and on to Taiwan, Singapore, Malaysia, and even the United States. Any belief system that has survived so well for so long in so many diverse settings compels respect.

THE PHILOSOPHY OF *FENG SHUI*:

INTRODUCTION:

Taoism is the philosophy of *Feng Shui*.

One of the foundation texts of Taoism, the *I Ching*, is especially influential.

From the Taoist belief in oneness (See "Oneness" in the "The Philosophy of Taoism – Metaphysics") comes the idea that we are all a part of *one* reality, which includes the earth and the heavens. As such, it is wise to live in peaceful coexistence within this mega system. *Feng Shui* supports this harmonic convergence.

In the macrocosm, this means maintaining a dynamic balance (See the previous section on *yin-yang*) with the flow of matter and energy through time-space. To Taoists, this means returning to the Tao (See *"Fu"* under The Philosophy of Taoism – Metaphysics").

In the microcosm, this means being aware of, and selective about, the placement of man-made objects in our personal and business surroundings. Hence the value of the principles and practices of *Feng Shui*.

THE THREE C'S:

We can begin to understand *Feng Shui* through three "C's" that I believe form the philosophic structure of *Feng Shui*. They are: *chi*, connectedness, and consequences. An explanation of each follows:

CHI:

The first and most celebrated philosophic concept of *Feng Shui* is the influence of *chi* (See the previous section). *Chi* is the cosmic energy that permeates the universe. Picture the moon, the sun, the stars, the world, and every one and every thing on it as a vast, swirling stream of energy flowing through time and space. At any given moment and place, there is a unique configuration of that great energy-matter flux. *Feng Shui* is about the optimization of that endless stream.

Within a structure, the goal is to *circulate* the local *chi*. It should not flow straight through. So if two windows are directly across from each other, some diversion should be put between them to disperse and swirl the *chi*.

CONNECTEDNESS:

A second "C" of *Feng Shui* is one central to Taoism and many spiritual traditions. It is the notion that everything connects to everything else in some way, however distant. In modern times, this notion has been called *the butterfly effect*. The symbolism is that the flapping of a butterfly's wings in one part of the world could set into motion a chain of events that could cause a violent storm in another.

We witness physical connectivity every day in many ways. There are countless examples: The connectivity of matter and air molecules can transmit a sound great distances. A Luna Moth can detect the fragrance of his lady across a small town, and make a very long flight to reach her. (How charmingly like us men.) Shock waves from earthquakes can be registered around the world. Across 186,000 miles, the moon's gravity creates the massive tidal action on the Earth. From 93 million miles away, the sun stimulates the development of Vitamin D in us.

Connectivity goes far beyond the physics of mechanical and electromagnetic forces. There is really no limit to it.

Think of the power of an idea. Through invisible connections in the tapestry of time and space, the wisdom of the masters from 2500 years ago, comes to us, and profoundly influences our thinking and behavior today. And then there are the mysterious workings of quantum physics. Growing evidence indicates that things are so connected that our thoughts influence the outcome of laboratory experiments.

CONSEQUENCES:

Introduction:

The third "C" of *Feng Shui* is that there are consequences. How we bring our human and material elements together matters. Arrangements affect the flow of *chi*, and in turn, our personal and financial success.

Consequences for the Human Element:

The astrological aspect of *Feng Shui* places great significance on the exact time and place of an individual's birth. My interpretation of this notion is that the configuration of the specific energy stream of time-space surrounding a person's birth inextricably and permanently influences their nature, behavior, and entire life destiny.

Note: The operative word here is *influences*, not *determines*. We are creatures of free will. We are not predestined to an unalterable fate. If we were, there would be no sense in even attempting to improve our surroundings with such disciplines as *Feng Shui*.

By studying the time and place of our birth, the *Feng Shui* master can identify the predominant energy that underpins our life. She can then render a destiny reading. This is not a prediction about how a person *will* fare in the stream of life, but rather a description of the stream itself. Understanding the course ahead – with all of its potential risks and rewards – can help us avoid the rocks, navigate the rapids, and take advantage of the friendly currents. We can better enjoy the beauty and adventure of our great voyage through life.

Feng Shui destiny readings provide advice on the following areas: lucky and unlucky times; nature and character; personal relationships; professional development; and business and investment decisions.

Consequences for the Material Element:

A popular image of *Feng Shui* is one of orienting material things – objects, furniture, and buildings – with the surrounding environment.

What things we bring together, and how they relate to each other is relevant to how well we function with them.

Man-made objects affect the flow of *Chi* in helpful ways to create beneficial *Feng Shui*, and in harmful ways to create deleterious *Feng Shui*. The intelligent inclusion and juxtaposition of elements - large and small, external and internal – allows for the unblocked and uncomplicated flow of *chi*. *By* harmonizing with this flow, we struggle less, and achieve more. We are naturally more smooth and graceful. We find it easier to resolve conflicts, to be at peace, to see clearly, to find meaning and direction, to maintain health and vigor, to be productive, to achieve professional and financial success, and to develop successful relationships. In short, the unimpeded flow of *chi* increases our chances of good fortune.

THE PRACTICE OF *FENG SHUI*:

OVERVIEW:

In general, *Feng Shui* practitioners seek to understand the terrain and judge its suitability for the purpose and function of a residence, retail space, office building, factory, road, bridge, utility, or infrastructure. They analyze the relationships of the human and material elements to the environment. They then apply the principles of *Feng Shui* to design or redesign a structure to optimize the flow of *chi*. The ideal result is a project that efficiently and effectively achieves the intended purpose in harmony with nature and the Tao.

DISCOVERY:

What follows are three very fundamental and critical discovery or fact-gathering steps in the practice of *Feng Shui*. Those readers familiar with the legalities of performance contracts might consider this the *due diligence* part of a *Feng Shui* service provider's job. These axioms are presented in reverse chronological order to better make the point.

Form Follows Function:

The principle *form follows function* simply means that we need to first determine exactly what we want to do (function) with a home, office or factory *before* we can intelligently begin a design (form).

Function Follows Character:

Here is a thought that is rarely found in books on *Feng Shui*, much less those on interior design: An honest, deep, and comprehensive understanding of the nature and character of the owners and/or occupants even supercedes the function consideration in sequence and priority. Only when we understand the core human elements can we proceed with any assurance that what we design and build will be the right way for the life path of the owners or occupants.

This is the secret of enlightened *Feng Shui* practitioners. They know there is this important discovery process *even before* the basic question of intended function. We need to know our, or our clients, nature, needs, motives, values, interests, and intentions.

What good is exquisitely designing and constructing a building with *Feng Shui* principles only to realize too late that it is incongruent with the characters and interests of the occupants? So we must understand the essential character of the people associated with the project. Much of this understanding concerns values, priorities, and lifestyle. This requires interpersonal intelligence to see into the heart of a person. It also takes diplomacy to convince the client of change.

Character Follows Transformation:

The advanced discovery process continues as we probe deeper. What good is basing a design around a character when that character is misdirected, imbalanced, or troubled? A common example of this is the tendency to want to impress others with the size of our homes, and extravagance of our furnishings. How many structures are aesthetic "white elephants" or environmental travesties because of an egocentric owner? How many structures rapidly become functionally obsolete because the mercurial personality of the client? Good, strong values and stable character matter in a very practical sense.

Discovery Summary:

I believe it is only with the above multi-dimensional approach to the practice of *Feng Shui* can we fully optimize the flow of *chi*, and create good fortune in our life. Once again, wholeness is all.

Only when we truthfully assess our strengths and weaknesses; heal, correct, and balance ourselves; purify our intentions; and commit to our authentic, self-actualizing life can we achieve the very highest forms of *Feng Shui*, and congruence with the Tao.

Once again, the real starting point for all of our serious endeavors is our innermost being. First seek inner peace, and beautiful living will naturally follow.

FOCUS:

Feng Shui consultants recommend that rooms have a strong focal point. In my opinion, the reasoning behind this is that our subconscious mind is always on guard, monitoring and analyzing our surroundings for opportunities or dangers. When there is no focal point, there is no basis for our mind to make a determination. So it remains in an alert, anxious, energy-draining state until the security or opportunity issue is resolved. Obviously, an unfinished cognitive task is digressive in the least, and pathological at the worst. It is stressful to always be on high alert.

FLOW OF *CHI*:

Visualize Fluid Flow:

The building perspective of *Feng Shui* studies the invisible forms of energy that flow though, and become encapsulated within, structures. To understand the dynamics, it is helpful to visualize *chi* as a fluid in motion, much like air or water. Think of it flowing into a building and through its rooms. Then intuit what might facilitate and impede this flow.

To Enhance Flow:

To enhance the flow of *chi*, we include people, animals, plants, moving water, and bamboo flutes in a room. To reduce the flow of *chi* we include still pools of water, and strong, dense structures like foundations, walls, and rocks.

To Alter Speed:

To speed the flow of *chi*, we use *yang* elements. They are smooth, reflective, surfaces such as glass, mirrors, polished wood, glazed ceramics, and marble. To slow the flow of *chi*, we use dull, course, absorbing or protruding surfaces such as fabrics, unfinished wood, unglazed ceramics, course stone, and rugged rock.

YIN-YANG BALANCE:

One of the principles of *Feng Shui* is to balance *yin* and *yang* i.e., never have an excess of either. The following table illustrates conditions of excess of *yin* and *yang* to avoid or attenuate:

Excess *Yin*	Excess *Yang*
Very dark	Very bright
Grays and blues	Reds, oranges, and yellows
Silent	Loud
Damp and wet	Dry and parched
Narrow and closed	Voluminous and open

CORRESPONDENCE:

Introduction:

Taoism, and by extension *Feng Shui*, draws with logical consistency, a correlation between a person's inner world and outer world. What people keep in their living and work spaces reflects something about what is going on inside of them. The quantity and quality of their personal belongings, decorations, and furniture makes some kind of a statement about them.

Hesitations:

But before we start taking readings on a person's space and making any hasty generalizations about them, two qualifications are in order. First, it is important to remember budgetary restrictions. Few of us are able to equip and decorate a space without any regard to cost. Second, many hold a kind consideration for the needs and tastes of others frequenting their space. So they compromise their wishes for others. This changes the dynamic of the inner-outer correspondence. With those two provisos in mind, here are some further thoughts:

Clarity:

Those who are clear in their inner life tend to be clear in their outer life; and vice versa.

People who are clear about who they are and what their life is about mirror this clarity in their surroundings. They scrupulously avoid things that are digressive and damaging, and they never tolerate clutter for very long.

Their belongings are few, simple, unostentatious, and utilitarian. They follow the simple rule: "*A place for everything, and everything in its place.*"

These types of people enjoy simple and natural delights. If they have memorabilia, inspirational, or spiritual items, they are never for pretentious display. And as precious as they may be, the loss of them is taken with a stoic indifference. They know that all material phenomena change, so they do not form unhealthy attachments with them.

Congestion:

People who are confused about who they are and what their life is about also mirror this confusion in their surroundings. These types of people fill their minds, bodies, and emotions with the superfluous and even the toxic. And so their dwellings are the same way. They lack stability and so does their surroundings. There is no strong direction or congruency inside so there is none outside. Confusion and chaos rules on both sides of their skin.

People who are not at peace and are not complete are always on the lookout for the next thing to give them a temporary high. They are a merchants dream, buying things far in excess of their actual needs. Instead of enjoying things for the moment, they have to own it. They must always have the latest fad or fashion.
They seek, grasp, attach, and hoar. They never let go of anything. (And a physical constipation often matches this material constipation.) Things come in the door, but don't go out. Over time their homes become a museum of pop cultural history.

They are surrounded with the unnecessary, the burdensome, and even the damaging. There is never enough, yet they don't have time to use or enjoy what they have.

Eventually, this insatiable, often compulsive, acquisition necessitates further acquisition - larger facilities to hold everything. At first this means more containers, shelves, cabinets, and dressers. Then comes the lease of mini storage facilities, room additions, and even the trade up to a larger home or office building. The inevitable result of this is predictable: After the collector/hoarder passes away, someone - usually a hapless relative - ends up with the unenviable task of disposing of it all.

The reason congestion is such an issue here is that it is anathema to the flow of *chi*.

THE FIVE ELEMENTS or PHASES AND *FENG SHUI*:

Wu-Hsing or The Five Elements covered in the previous section form an integral part of *Feng Shui*. The idea in their use is to design and promote conditions that allow the five to harmonize with each other and support the occupants.

The key is balance. While all five elements should be represented in a home, the needs of the primary occupant of any one room (the one who "owns" it) should be considered in the detailed placement of them.

TOOLS:

With the *I Ching* as its philosophic basis, *Feng Shui* practitioners employ three basic tools: *The Magic Square*, the *Pa-Gua Octagon*, and the *Lo P'an Compass*.

A detailed explanation of each of these would require volumes of technical explanation. What follows is a brief introduction. The actual use of these tools, especially the *Lo P'an* compass, can become very complex. The inquisitive reader should find a reputable "how to" *Feng Shui* text, and consult an expert on this high art.

THE *LO SHU* SQUARE / MAGIC SQUARE:

Introduction:

History is necessarily conjectural. Who with great certainty knows the truth of distant origins about anything?

According to one ancient legend, the Shaman-King Ta-Yu ("Yu the Great") noticed markings on the shell of a turtle on the bank of the Lo River. He discovered the numbers 1-9 arranged in the below 3 x 3 grid. This matrix became known as *The Lo Shu Square* or *The Magic Square* because any row or column of numbers sums to 15.

4	9	2
3	5	7
8	1	6

Qualities:

The Magic Square is more than just a mathematical curiosity. Here are some of its other important qualities:

The even *Lo Shu* numbers are *yin*. The odd numbers are *yang*. Counting sequentially from one to nine creates *yin-yang* cycles.

Even *yin* numbers are in the corners. Odd *yang* numbers are in the cardinal or primary compass points.

The sequence of the *Lo Shu* numbers indicates the directions of energy movement within any system. This pattern repeats over time, so is predictable. This key insight is a major factor in *Feng Shui* practice.

THE PA K'UA / BA GUA:

Introduction:

The Magic Square is the basis for one of the most commonly used tools of *Feng Shui* - the *Pa K'ua* (older name) or *Ba Gua* (newer name). *Ba* means eight, and *gua* means trigrams or outcomes.

The eight trigrams of the *Ba Gua* are created by the interaction of *yin* and *yang*, and are usually displayed as an octagon. Each side of the octagon is associated with a trigram (see below), a compass point, an element, an aspect of life (career, knowledge, helpful people, etc.) and other qualities.

The *Pa K'ua* is also depicted like the Magic Square as a 3 x 3 grid. It is sometimes called the *Palace of Nine Halls* with a hall for each of the eight directions and a ninth hall (number five) as the center courtyard.

Note: In the Chinese tradition, the south compass point is oriented at the top of the octagon – opposite that used in the West.

In the East, the *Ba Gua* has been used for thousands of years to inform the design of new structures and to enhance the energy flow in existing structures.

In the West, G. W. Leibniz studied the theoretical basis of the *Ba Gua* when he developed the principles of binary arithmetic. There are other (often "spooky") parallels between the process that developed the *Ba Gua* and modern physics. And as we will see later, Dr. Carl Jung's studies in this area influenced his thinking on his notion of synchronicity.

In both the East and the West, *Feng Shui* practitioners overlay a plot of land, a home, a room, or even a work surface with the *Ba Gua* template. They then arrange objects and structures to eliminate blockages to *chi* and to optimize the flow of *chi*.

The principles behind, and the application of, the *Ba Gua* can become very complex. There are many different interpretations, approaches, tools, schools, and situations. But the common fundamental purpose in its use is much the same as this book's: *to achieve inner peace and beautiful living.*

What follows is a cursory overview of the *Ba Gua* and its constituent elements. Serious students of this ancient tool should consult an advanced text and seek study under a *Feng Shui* master.

<u>The Symbols of Lines:</u>

Only two types of lines are used to create the trigrams of the *Pa K'ua* and the hexagrams of the *I Ching*: *yin* and *yang*. The *yin* element is represented by a broken line (__ __). The *yang* element is represented by a continuous solid line (____).

The universe is constantly changing. Whenever a *yang* force reaches its fullest power and dominates an area, it begins to weaken and slowly gives way to its *yin* opposite. Remember that both *yin* and *yang* are always present. So "old *yang*" (two solid lines) turns to "young *yin*" (lower broken line, upper solid line).

The first (bottom) line on a trigram or hexagram indicates the trend of the change. Also, the bottom line is symbolic for the Earth; the middle line for humans; and the upper line for heaven.

Trigrams:

The creation of the *Pau Kua* trigrams is attributed to the legendary Chinese Emperor Fu Hsi. The trigrams of the *Pa K'ua* consist of three *yin* or *yang* lines stacked one upon the other. They are *read from the bottom up*.

When three *yin* and *yang* lines are stacked to form a trigram, eight (2 to the 3rd power) different combinations of *yin-yang* lines are possible.

Each trigram is a symbolic representation of a phase or state of transition in time and space of all natural phenomena including human behavior.

Hexagrams:

When the binary outcome of *yin* or *yang* lines is repeated six times to form a hexagram of stacked lines, 64 (2 to the 6th power) different possible combinations of lines result. These 64 hexagrams form the *I Ching* system. Associated with each hexagram are combinations of the five elements and other natural phenomenal that symbolize dynamic qualities of life such as creativity, receptivity, difficulties, etc.

When considered by a sincere seeker, these symbols stimulate transformational energies, and are the basis of the oracle (See "Divination" under "The Philosophy of Taoism – Metaphysics"). Purity of intent is necessary in this divinational process. (It is not meant to maximize the return in financial markets or to beat the odds in gambling.) It works best when the subject is considering an emotionally charged issue with uncertain outcomes.

Two "Heavens":

There are two basic *Ba Gua* octagonal arrangements. One is called "Early Heaven" (*Hsien Tien* or *Xian Tien*), the other "Later Heaven" *(Hu Tien* or *Hou Tien).* This "Later Heaven" design is related to the Magic Square.

"Early Heaven":

This ancient arrangement is credited to Fu Hsi. It depicts reality before the existence of the world. This is the *yin* Feng Shui. The all *yin K'un* trigram is oriented north (bottom). The all *yang Chien* trigram is oriented south (top). Early Heaven aims at balancing human and natural forces, and was originally used to locate gravesites. True to its *yin* description, it is passive or unchanging.

"Later Heaven":

King Wen, the founder of the Chou (Zhou) Dynasty (1027-1024), developed the "Later Heaven" *Ba Gua* arrangement. It depicts reality after the world came into existence. This is the *yang Feng Shui. K'an,* the *yin – yang - yin* trigram is oriented north (bottom). *Li,* the *yang – yin - yang* trigram is south (top). The Later Heaven version relies heavily on the *I Ching* and depicts *chi* in motion.

The tables below provide the trigram name, trigram structure, *Lo Shu* Number, element, and where applicable animal associated with each of the cardinal compass points of the "Later Heaven" *Ba Gua.*

Overview:

Compass Direction	Trigram Name	Trigram Structure (From bottom up)
South (top)	*Li*	*Yang-yin-yang*
Southwest	*K'un / Kun*	*Yin-yin-yin*
West (right)	*Lui / Tui / Dui*	*Yang-yang-yin*
Northwest	*Chien / Chyan*	*Yang-yang-yang*
North (bottom)	*K'an / Kan*	*Yin-yang-yin*
Northeast	*Ken*	*Yin-yin-yang*
East (left)	*Chen / Jen*	*Yang-yin-yin*
Southeast	*Sun / Hsun*	*Yin-yang-yang*

South (Top):

Trigram Name	*Li*
Trigram Form (bottom up)	*Yang-yin-yang*
Lo Shu Number	9
Element	Fire
Animal	Red Phoenix (Bird)

Southeast:

Trigram Name	*Sun / Hsun*
Trigram Form (bottom up)	*Yin-yang-yang*
Lo Shu Number	4
Element	Wood

East (Left):

Trigram Name	*Chen / Jen / Zhen*
Trigram Form (bottom up)	*Yang-yin-yin*
Lo Shu Number	3
Element	Wood
Animal	Green Dragon

Northeast:

Trigram Name	Ken / Gen
Trigram Form (bottom up)	*Yin-yin-yang*
Lo Shu Number	8
Element	Earth

North (Bottom):

Trigram Name	*K'an / Kan*
Trigram Form (bottom up)	*Yin-yang-yin*
Lo Shu Number	1
Element	Water
Animal	Black Turtle

Northwest:

Trigram Name	*Chien / Chyan / Quian*
Trigram Form (bottom up)	*Yang-yang-yang*
Lo Shu Number	6
Element	Metal

West (Right):

Trigram Name	*Lui / Tui / Dui*
Trigram Form (bottom up)	*Yang-yang-yin*
Lo Shu Number	7
Element	Metal
Animal	White Tiger

Southwest:

Trigram Name	*K'un / Kun*
Trigram Form (bottom up)	*Yin-yang-yin*
Lo Shu Number	2
Element	Earth

THE *LO P'AN* (*LOU-PAN*) GEOMANTIC COMPASS:

The third main tool in *Feng Shui* is the *Lo P'an* (everything bowl) Compass. *Feng Shui geomancers* use the *Lo P'an* to determine the desirability of specific locations. This complex and powerful instrument is a magnetic needle surrounded by concentric rings containing vast amounts of condensed information. The *I Ching's Pa K'ua* is at its center, but there is much more. There can be 4 to 40 rings of information with up to 365 segments in each ring. Some Chinese geomancers claim it contains all the important secrets of the Earth.

Masters analyze and correlate the wisdom of the 64 *I Ching* hexagrams (*yin-yang* divisions); the five elements described earlier; planets; stars; constellations; signs of the Zodiac; and other variables with the nature and direction of local energies. This instrument is used to diagnoses illnesses, forecast business, and locate propitious sites for everything from homes to skyscrapers.

> Note: Here is yet another question to investigate: Is there a correlation between the principles and practices of *Feng Shui* and the mystical influences of astrology?

FENG SHUI SCHOOLS:

Historians suspect that *Feng Shui* was first used to properly locate burial sites. This gave rise to the *Form School* of *Feng Shui*. The practice evolved to home, shops, roads, bridges, factories, dams and other structures.

The focus on the interior and furnishings of buildings

and how they affect the flow of *chi* gave rise to many other approaches to *Feng Shui* that are in use today. Some texts group all non-form schools under the classification *Compass Schools,* referring to their references to compass directions. Some smaller schools developed around the style of one particular master.

It is not uncommon for books on *Feng Shui* to differ on their presentations of the types and number of schools. What follows is an overview of the more common ones.

THE FORM, LANDFORM or ENVIRONMENTAL (*XINGFA*) SCHOOL:

Introduction:

The Form or Landform School is the oldest form of *Feng Shui* practice. Its name derives from the physical features of the land such as the mountains, contours, valleys, rivers, and the exteriors of man-made structures (they are viewed as a landform). It uses the five elements as descriptors.

Landform *Feng Shui* is a visual, common sense approach that focuses on the *chi* that freely flows outdoors. It often describes land in terms of mountains and water. A mountain devoid of water is excessively static (*yin*). Water devoid of mountain is excessively dynamic (*yang*). Once again the idea is to have both in balance.

The ancient Chinese were dependent upon the land, and vulnerable to the changes in nature. They sought a system that would allow them to minimize their risks, and make better decisions about the when and where of life, especially agriculture. They studied the patterns, cycles, and effects of nature to learn how they changed in hopes of developing a method of forecasting. Most apparent was the seasons. *Yang* grew in spring and peaked in summer. *Yin* increased in fall and peaked in winter.

Form School Animals:

The Form School uses animals with colorful names to describe the desired topography in the four cardinal compass directions (north, south, east, west). In addition, there is also the *mountain dragon* (complete with head, spine, legs, and claws) that creates an energy flow over a mountain. The path it takes is a *dragon vein*.

Here are the four primary animal symbols, which summarize the ideal positioning of a structure in the Form School:

North - *The Black Turtle:*

The hard shell of *The Black Turtle* symbolizes solidity, stability, security, and longevity. It is comforting to live in the hills or next to a mountain that shelters your back from cold northerly wind. If there are elevation differences, the higher ground is always in the rear or north.

East- *The Green Dragon:*

The Green Dragon holds spiritual qualities of far-sightedness and wisdom. It protects the left or east of the structure. Dragons should not have sharp edges or cliffs. It is always on higher ground than *The White Tiger* (next). In Chinese culture, the dragon represents good fortune.

West - *The White Tiger:*

The White Tiger embodies physical strength. Sun and shade are in balance. The breezes are gentle. The hills are rolling. The soil is rich. Vegetation is lush. It reminds us of the violent part of our nature that exists for defense and attack.

South - *The Red Phoenix*:

The Red Phoenix never dies. It represents an inspirational and exciting forward vision. It is the sentry in the front or south, which is low to the ground to allow an unobstructed view.

THE EAST-WEST (EIGHT MANSIONS) SCHOOL:

Introduction:

The method of this school of *Feng Shui* is simple and fun. It is based on the belief that each person and every building has four favorable and four unfavorable compass directions. Seeking the favorable and avoiding the unfavorable directions for a given activity allows a person to perform efficiently and to have better luck. By knowing propitious directions, a person can be in sync with, and supported by, a particular floor plan. Since each direction or area covers a different activity in life, no one direction is better than another. See the "The Basic Eight *Pa K'ua* Trigrams" tables above for the correspondence of activity with direction.

East-West Groups:

The two sets of four directions are classified into East and West groups as follows:

Group	Numbers	Favorable Compass Directions
East	3, 4, 9, 6	East, Southeast, South, and Northwest
West	2. 7. 8, 1	West, Southwest, North, and Northeast

To which group an individual belongs depends on

their year of birth and gender. For buildings, it depends on its direction or orientation.

Any complete book on *Feng Shui* will provide a table that links years of birth and gender to a number. This number can also be calculated as follows:

For Women:

Add the last two numbers of the birth year. If it is over ten, add the two digits. Then add five. Again if it is over ten, add the two digits. Example for a woman who was born in 1979: 7 + 9 = 16. 1 + 6 = 7. 7 + 5 = 12. 1 + 2 = 3. Three is the number, therefore east is her group.

For Men:

Add the last two numbers of the birth year. If it is over ten, add the two digits. Subtract from ten. Example for a man born in 1942: 4 + 2 = 6. 10 − 6 = 4. Four is the number, therefore east is his group. For a man born in 1984: 8 + 4 = 12. 1 + 2 = 3. 10 − 3 = 7. Seven is the number, therefore west is his group.

THE FLYING STAR SCHOOL:

The Flying Star School can become very complex. It is not intuitive. It is based on the belief that each direction exerts a different energy. It uses the Five Elements, the *Lo Shu* Magic Square, the *Pa Qua* Octagon, and the *Lo P'an* Compass. It is named "Flying Star" because the numbers of the *Lo Shu* Magic Square symbolize stars and they move or "fly" in a specific directional sequence within the matrix. This floating attribute is an attempt to adjust to the way conditions change over time. Additionally, each cell within the *Lo Shu* is called a *palace*, so it is called *The Nine Palaces*.

The Flying Star School uses the tools and techniques of the East-West School, but extends them considerably. It adds seasons of the year, members of the family, organs of the body, etc. This approach honors the preeminence of energy and how its pattern of movement changes in a predictable manner.

Readers interested in this approach to *Feng Shui* should consult an authoritative reference, which has sufficient detail to describe the different arrangements of the "stars" as they "fly", and what these movements mean.

THE BLACK HAT SECT (BHS) or TANTRIC BUDDHIST SCHOOL or WESTERN *FENG SHUI*:

The Black Hat Sect (BHS) is the most recent of the *Feng Shui* schools designed to accommodate the needs of society today. Professor Thomas Lin Yun of Berkeley California developed this approach as an amalgam of Taoism, traditional *Feng Shui,* and Tibetan Buddhism. He adapted it to American culture, and it has grown in popularity since he brought it from Taiwan in 1986.

The BHS is very spiritual. The central idea is to use human powers (science, psychology, philosophy, spirituality, etc.) to work in cooperation with the highest power (*The One, The Spirit*) to design optimum conditions for the flow of both visible and invisible *chi.* The BHS *Feng Shui* practitioner becomes a limited partner of sorts in a joint venture with God.

The BHS dramatically departs with the above schools by ignoring compass directions. Instead of using the *Lo P'an* magnetic compass, each house is analyzed from the perspective of its main door, and each room from its interior door. The *Ba Gua* is then used as a template with its career area or *gua* oriented with the door instead of north. Hence the distinction between the *Ba Gua* the *Pa K'ua*. These two methods of orientation are considered equally valid. All other features associated with the octagon of the *Ba Gua* then align from there. So the direction of the different activities of life will change with the orientation of the door of each structure.

THE INTUITIVE SCHOOL:

Those who rely primarily on their intuitive powers to practice *Feng Shui* believe this emphasis is sufficient to distinguish it as a separate school. Traditionalists in the field disagree. They argue that the intuitive approach still employs the same well-established rules of *Feng Shui*.

IN SUMMARY:

The preceding *Descriptions* briefly sketched the fundamentals, the tools, and the schools of *Feng Shui*. The main goal, once again, is to fully optimize the flow of *chi* to create good fortune in our personal and professional life.

In the practice of *Feng Shui*, I have emphasized the importance of function, character and transformation. This character-based start to the application of *Feng Shui* is not typical in the literature. But I believe that only when we truthfully assess our strengths and weaknesses, heal and balance ourselves, purify our intentions, and commit to an authentic life can we achieve the highest forms of *Feng Shui* and congruence with the Tao. Wholeness is all.

Once again, the real starting point for all of our serious endeavors is our innermost being. First seek inner peace, and beautiful living will naturally follow.

PRESCRIPTIONS:

BECOME FAMILIAR WITH *FENG SHUI*:

You do not have to become an expert. Just get to know the basic concepts, tools, perspectives, and schools of *Feng Shui*. Read an authoritative book on the subject. Take a class or seminar. Consider joining or even starting a *Feng Shui* special interest group. I once attended a *Feng Shui* club meeting at a local bookstore. It is surprising what you can learn from the different experiences of laymen.

SEEK PROFESSIONAL GUIDANCE:

If you plan to invest a significant amount of time, effort, and resources into a real estate development, consider seeking the advice of a reputable *Feng Shui* consultant. Check their credentials, experiences, and references. Have they apprenticed with a master? Have they become familiar with Taoism and Chinese culture? Are they patient and open to your questions? Can they explain their recommendations in a way that you understand?

Will they be there to witness the results of their advice?

Be careful in the selection of a *Feng Shui* school. Do not get caught up in new age embellishments like incense, crystals, mirrors, bamboo, geometric objects, flutes, or statues. Seek someone who has a proven record of enhancing lives with time-tested traditional *Feng Shui*.

Remember that *Feng Shui* works with only five elements: earth, wood, fire, metal and water.

THINK INTUITIVELY:

Use your intuitive intelligence in the application of *Feng Shui*. Review the Taoist principle of *wu-wei* under its ethical philosophy. Do not force. This should not be hard work. It should flow and evolve naturally.

THINK TELEOLOGICALLY:

Remember form follows function and function follows character.

First, last, and always, think about *teleology* or purpose. What is the intended use of the existing or proposed structure? What functions will it support? For how long? Are the stated functions really beneficial over time, or just passing fancies?

These and other soul-searching questions are critical in your initial analysis. An honest look at your intentions can save many years, and much money in future content and structural adjustments and changes.

THINK HOLISTICALLY:

Introduction:

If you are designing or remodeling a home, office building, or even factory, begin with the big picture. Get the *gestalt* of the project. This is one of the most important decisions in a building project. Here are three basic considerations to begin your checklist:

Climate:

How many sunny and how many cloudy days are there in the year? What is the path across the property of the rise and fall of the sun? What does the annual chart of temperature, humidity, and precipitation look like? What is the prevailing wind velocity and direction? What are the lowest winter temperature and wind chill readings, and how long do they last?

Terrain:

What is the geological stability and hazards? What are the significant features of the terrain? What is the property elevation and how does that affect functionality? What is the composition of the soil? Does the ground support your purpose? Could drainage be a problem? Are you in a flood plain? How might existing and future infrastructure and municipal projects impact the project? (In California, developers remove the tops of hills. In Florida the draining of aquifers creates huge sink holes.)

Surroundings:

Are there too few or too many people? What are the demographics and what are the population trends? Is the present residential, commercial, industrial, and public infrastructure compatible? What are the local animal and plant conditions? (In Wisconsin, geese can soil otherwise pristine walks around ponds and lakes. In Florida, red tide, insects, and reptiles can ruin your whole day.)

THINK DEFENSIVELY:

Introduction:

Promoters and project managers often get caught up in the exciting possibilities of a real estate development. Be patient. Take time to study and minimize your risks. An initial, minimal, cautionary analysis could save your entire investment, not to mention your peace of mind. Here are some of the risk questions to investigate:

Past:

What is the history of the land and/or building? Here are some historical possibilities – however remote – that you should uncover before investing time, energy, and resources: Examples: Indian burial grounds; toxic and nuclear waste spills (Remember *Times Beach* and *Bhopal*); suicides; homicides; genocides; mud slides; floods; earthquakes; hurricanes; tornados; sinkholes, and invasions of both pests and people. Spiritualists believe that the energy from both good and evil remain in structures. Highly sensitive mystics claim to sense the vibrations of events years or even decades after they occurred. Could this be the explanation for angel and ghost sightings?

Present:

Investigate the current risk factors. Do *shars* ("poison arrows") exist in or outside the structure? Are the forms of driveways, sidewalks, and roads or nearby structures threatening?

Stand in the existing or proposed front door. How do you feel? Mitigate any *shars* by covering them with plants or other structures so they are not in sight.

In some locations, uranium occurs naturally in the earth and breaks down over time forming radioactive ions. Long exposure to this *radon* from underground water, soil, and rocks eventually can cause birth defects and leukemia. Radon is the neutron bomb of home ownership. It can kill people while leaving the building intact. Does the property have this risk?

Who are your neighbors? Are they the type of people with whom you are comfortable? What are the chances of noise from parties, arguments, radios, equipment, and vehicles?

What is the traffic pattern and activities surrounding

the property? At the outer perimeter, is the property in range of an installation that has a potential chemical, biological, or nuclear threat? If so, how safe is their operation? (Recall *Three Mile Island*) How vulnerable are these sensitive installations to a terrorist attack? Are there electric power transformers, lines, or towers in the area with electromagnetic radiation that can cause cell or neurological damage? What other visible or hidden threats exist?

Future:

What is the community plan? Is there a major residential or industrial development on the drawing boards? If so, how compatible is it with your vision? What are the chances of transportation authorities building a street or major thoroughfare, and possibly taking your property in the process?

**ADVENTURES IN *FENG SHUI*
THE STORY OF THE UNEXPECTED HIGHWAY**

I knew a gentle farmer who lived peacefully with his wife on his Wisconsin farm most all his life. But then they put in a highway right next to his property. Throughout the rest of his life, he was tormented by the traffic noise.

IN GENERAL:

Here are some general questions to consider before buying an existing property or before starting a new development:

Have you taken an unemotional, objective view of the proposed acquisition? Have you let your enthusiasm blind you to the negatives of a property or project?

Are there any natural or man-made risks or threats in the area?

Does the social style, and economic climate support your interests, goals, and lifestyle?

Review the positioning and orientation of the building. As questions such as this: Will the sun fall where you want it to through the day? Will the rain from severe storms drain away from the property, and not flood the interior?

Are the materials in the building safe, non-toxic, biodegradable, recyclable, and sustainable?

Is the building structurally sound and aesthetically pleasing? Does it appear top-heavy, or similar to some threatening object? Does it blend well with the surroundings, like it belongs there?

Does the building fully support the current and future intended uses? Is it functionally effective?

Is the building and appliances energy efficient and low maintenance?

Does the construction plans meet or exceed the requirements of the local building codes? Will code inspectors ensure that this will happen?

Does your builder have a reputation for quality work and for correcting any defects in a timely manner?

Are any remedies currently in order? Remember that no place is perfect. Is it desirable and practical to nullify any negative features with *Feng Shui* countermeasures?
Refer to a professional text and/or consultant for which ones are appropriate for your condition.

THE SITE:

An ideal site is one protected by hills, trees, bushes or even buildings without impeding a good view. (Remember the "Animals" previously discussed.)

Do not build in the center of a T-junction or at the end of a cul-de-sac. The linear flow of *chi* becomes trapped there.

Do not build on land that is triangular since that creates negative *karma*.

A straight road can lead to the building. The drive leading to the front entrance can be straight or have a gentle curve. It should never abruptly take a sharp turn.

Do not orient the building so that it is vulnerable to neighboring structures. Avoid being the target of other buildings that seem to point toward it like a *secret arrow*.

Try to orient the building so that it is facing south. Ideally the view should be to an open space of land, a valley, or a body of water (best) like a pond, lake or sea. If there is a slope, the back should be higher than the front. *Chi* should flow freely up the slope to the entrance. It is preferable to be between two hills; the one to the left (East) being slightly taller.

To conserve *chi*, build a pool of water or a fishpond. Ideally, arrange for a stream or river to run along one side of the structure, move in front of it so that *Chi* can access the entrance, and then flow off in the distance. The bends and curves should be graceful to ensure that the *chi* does not overflow the boundaries. The best is a gentle, meandering path.

THE UTILITIES:

Utilities are an often-overlooked health risk.

Water:

Have your water tested. If it is questionable, buy high quality bottled water or use a filtering system. If you use such a system, make sure you change the filter on schedule or it will trap contaminants and actually make your water worse.

Gas:

Check for leaks. Natural gas is odorless. Gas companies actually add the odor to the gas to make it detectible by smell. If you have a home or building with a basement, check for *radon* gas.

Electrical Utility Lines:

Wires should not be suspended above your property so they could fall on it during a storm. Wiring should be up to code, and never overloaded.

Electromagnetic Radiation (EMR):

As mentioned earlier, be mindful of basic physics. A current passing through a conductor produces electromagnetic radiation. Our nervous system is an incredibly complex electrical system with connections to every muscle, organ (brain and heart), and cell in our body. It generates its own electromagnetic radiation (EMR) field. Electromagnetic fields near our brain can easily disrupt and damage this vital system. People living near power lines complain of weariness, poor memory, headaches, and other health problems. Studies around the world indicate that prolonged exposure to EMR weakens the immune system, compromises health, and may even be carcinogenic. Children who live near high-voltage lines have a higher risk of cancer in general and leukemia in particular. NEVER live near high-powered electrical lines, especially ones that emit a constant humming noise.

**ADVENTURES IN *FENG SHUI*
THE STORY OF MY ELECTRICIAN FRIEND**

One of my best friends from my youth was an electrician who worked around EMR. At the time, he was relatively young and in top shape. But he began to suffer from abdominal pains. Exploratory surgery found inoperable cancer spread throughout his body. He tragically died an early death.

THE LANDSCAPE:

We transition to or from our home or office through the surrounding landscape. It is a portal that both introduces us to, and buffers us from, the outside world. Ask how you want this transition to occur, and how you want this portal to function. Consider the use of walls, fences, arches, rocks, stones, flowers, plants, scrubs, trees, paths, bridges, miniature buildings, statues, pools, streams, fountains, and lighting to create your own magical wonderland.

THE BUILDING INTERIOR:

Below is a checklist of building interior issues listed in alphabetical order:

Air Quality and Pollutants:

Check to ensure that the following indoor air pollutants are not present in your place: carbon monoxide, sulfur dioxide, vinyl chloride, synthetic materials, aerosol sprays, toiletries, incoming fireplace or barbecue smoke, out-gassing building materials (glues, carpets, shelving), pesticide sprays, cleaning supplies, paint supplies, hydrocarbon fuels, dust, mites, molds, pollens, bacteria, viruses, garbage, natural gas, gasoline, and car exhaust.

Air Quality and Systems:

Do not assume that a healthy supply of the most basic requirement for life – air - is assured. In many cities, outdoor air is hazardous to your health. And indoor air pollution has been estimated to be a five times greater risk. The air problems in factories can be apparent, or can be hidden as in the case of asbestos. But consider modern high-rise office buildings. (On a much smaller scale the following applies to homes.) Where older office buildings had windows that opened, the newer ones do not. They rely exclusively on computerized, power-dependent central heating and air conditioning systems. These A/C systems have great advantages. But they can also circulate particles, allergens, fungus, mold, pathogens, bacteria, and viruses from just one person or source to all occupants in the building. (Recall *Legionnaires Disease*.) There is also the obvious vulnerability to biological, chemical, or even nuclear terrorism. Then there is power, computer, and equipment failures, which can and do occur. Without windows that open, how are hazards ventilated, and equipment failures handled? Consider these risks when you occupy, buy, or build residential or commercial real estate.

Asbestos:

In existing buildings, check for asbestos ceiling and floor tiles, insulation (especially around heating and air conditioning equipment), and air contamination. If this material exists, immediately contact a licensed asbestos removal serviceman for a full inspection.

Have it encapsulated or removed. Asbestos is a well-known carcinogen.

Bedroom:

Since you are vulnerable when asleep, orient your bed away from the door in a safe, secure place.

Candles:

Any type of lighting is very *yang*. Use candles or lights in dark rooms, halls, and corners where *chi* is trapped

Ceiling Beams:

Heavy beams too close to the occupants of a room can seem oppressive. Higher beams do not convey this sense of heaviness. Paint that makes the beams blend in to the ceiling can be an effective countermeasure to an existing condition.

Chimes:

Wind chimes echo *feng* (wind). You can use metal or bamboo chimes. Choose one with a melodious pleasant tone rather than one that jangles nerves.

Cleaning / Laundry Products:

This is one of the most common sources of toxic chemicals in the home. They are harmful and dangerous, especially to toddlers. There is no need to use them. There are very effective, harmless biodegradable cleaners on the market.

Clutter:

Clutter is abhorrent. It depletes *chi*. Get rid of it!

Colors:

Remember that colors create moods. Blue calms. Yellow is cheerful. Red excites. In China, the color red symbolizes warmth, happiness, and good luck. Colors such as green raise energy.

Doors:

Ideally, doors should allow an unrestricted view of the entire room. If it opens to a long passageway (a *corridor effect*), you can slow down the flow of *chi* with the use of hanging plants or ceiling lights.

Electrical Appliances:

Always maintain a safe distance from the potential hazards of spurious radiation from lamps, radios, televisions, audio equipment, computers, and especially microwave ovens. Check out or discard any source that is questionable. *Never* use a microwave oven, which has a door with a questionable seal. (Besides, they alter the structure of food, and can destroy enzymes. Hospitals never use microwaves to warm blood before infusions. They alter the composition of the blood.)

Flooring:

Why install chemically treated wool carpets or synthetic petroleum-based fiber carpets? Not only are they a source of indoor air pollution, but also they are a repository for dust, dirt, food, spores, bacteria, mites and other unhealthy substances. Use wood, stone or any other natural material for floors. One of the best floor coverings is bamboo.

Focus:

Make sure that the first thing you see when you enter the building conveys the tone and theme you desire.

The front entrance should not face the upstairs stairway or the back door. Put a nature scene on the wall in front of the door to allow the flow of energy. The toilet should also not be in direct sight of entrance.

Front Entrance:

This is a critical indoor/outdoor feature. If you like to convey a warm welcome, take a good look at your entrance and see if it does the job.

Do not forget security. This includes lighting, locks, and a peephole. Do not have to entirely open the door in order to see who is there, or to converse. An intercom is ideal. Never have windows in or along side of a door near the inner lock.

Foundation:

Make sure the structure of your building is stable. Many *Feng Shui* consultants advise against supporting a building on columns. However, those used in traditional Japanese *Haiku* homes have several advantages: they are earth-friendly, allow building on slopes, eliminate problems with damp leaky basements, eliminate *radon* risk, and are flexible in earthquakes.

Cabinets:

Be careful of cabinets that are constructed with toxic adhesives and chemicals, or are preserved or treated with them.

Furniture:

Place furniture so that you are at ease, and not looking over your shoulder. Desks and beds should be in a control position facing the door. Diagonally across a corner is best.

Hallways:

Avoid dark, cramped, zigzag passageways that slow and stagnate the flow of *chi*.

Height:

If there are nearby structures, build high enough so that there is a view beyond them. Make sure the sky is clearly visible.

Insulation:

Foam insulation for walls and ceilings contain harmful volatile chemicals. Where practical, substitute natural insulation.

Kitchen:

An entrance should be visible when cooking. The refrigerator should not be conspicuous. (You will tend to overeat if it is.) Keep water elements (sink, refrigerator) apart from fire elements (range). They create a psychological conflict.

Lighting:

Use natural lighting as much as possible. Find an appropriate balance between light (*yang*) and dark (*yin*) for the functions in each area. Curtains and shades can help adjust the intensity.

Materials:

Use natural materials and products. Do not use man-made materials and components with chemicals that give off gases, or contain substances that are toxic or carcinogenic.

Objects:

In general, be discrete in the use of objects in *Feng Shui*. Do not have too many of them. Heavy objects convey stability, and can reduce stress.

Paint:

In older structures, be careful of lead-based paint. In new construction, use paint with natural ingredients. Better yet, don't use paint at all. There is nothing more beautiful than nature's products - wood and stone.

Plants:

There are multiple advantages to bringing nature into your home or office. Use plants to soften sharp edges and to energize dead areas. Use plants to freshen the air; the more green leaves the better. Use plants to offset the hostility of cold, slick man-made materials, and to bring a psychologically healthy color and aesthetic.

Potted plants add beauty, improve indoor air quality, slow the flow of *Chi*, and bring energy to dead areas. If you use flowers, live potted ones are preferable to cut. Resist the temptation to use artificial flowers, plants, and trees. They do not fool anyone, and they collect dust.

Reflecting Surfaces:

Introduction:

Reflecting surfaces of all types, but especially mirrors, receive, partially absorb, and reflect incoming energy. Mirrors of many different styles exist in the form of the *Ba Gua*. They can attract or repel *Chi*. They also alter our sense of distance.

Don'ts:

Do not position a mirror so that it reflects only part of your image and cuts you in half. Do not position mirrors opposite each other, opposite a bed, or opposite a door or window so that they reflect *chi* back outside. Be considerate of your neighbors.

Do's:

Use reflecting surfaces to alter out of balance distances.

Use *Ba Gua* mirrors as reminders and affirmations. The idea is to allow these devices to stimulate your thoughts toward the realization of peace, happiness, and prosperity.

Position reflecting surfaces to replace missing sections of the *Ba Gua,* to enliven dead areas, and in general to harmonize the energy of areas.

The ideal is to place a mirror in the center of an area. But a wall location will do. They are also used on floors and ceilings. You can see *Ba Gua* – shaped mirrors in many Chinese establishments, especially restaurants.

Reflect *shar chi* with mirrors, especially those in the shape of the *Ba Gua.*

They (more than one can be used) can be positioned outside to reflect shar "attacks" from an negative place such as a cemetery, electrical field, factory, disaster site, crime scene, etc.

They can be placed inside to counteract the effects of a door or long hall opening when your back is facing it. The idea is that the mirror catches the energy from someone entering.

Roofs:

Flat exteriors that slope upward from the front of the building are best because they allow *chi* to flow.

Seating:

A chair is like a human hand. The front conveys the sense of a hand held open; it's inviting. The back of a chair is like a hand held up; it is halting. Therefore, an inviting entrance should never open to the back of a chair. Positioning a chair so that a person's back is to a door can make them nervous.

Shapes:

Avoid any sharp, angular, hostile-shaped surfaces since they are threatening and discourage wealth. Round edges and curves help *chi* flow. Round columns are better than square, and are structurally more efficient.

Tables:

Round tables are a sign of good luck. Have an even number of chairs. One projects loneliness.

Wall Items:

Sayings, photos, pictures, and paintings can make opportunities endless. Keep them eye level.

Wallpaper:

Think twice before you install wallpaper. If you do, use the chemical-free type.

Windows:

Narrow windows equate to narrow minds and to limited opportunities. They must not slide, and must easily open all the way to provide a clear view of the sky. Seek a balance between too much light (excessive *yang*) and too little (excessive *yin*). Keep security in mind. Here is a novel idea: How about shutters that actually work?

FU (RETURN)

"Return is the movement of the Tao. Yielding is the way of the Tao. All things are born of being. Being is born of non-being." – Chapter 40 of the *Tao Te Ching*

DESCRIPTIONS:

INTRODUCTION:

In Taoist philosophy, the concept of *fu* ("return") refers to the way everything returns to its origin.

This concept is symbolized by hexagram 24 in the *Tao Te Ching*.

"Empty yourself of everything. Let the mind rest at peace. The ten thousand things rise and fall while the Self watches their return. They grow and flourish and then return to the source. Returning to the source is stillness, which is the way of nature.

The way of nature is unchanging. Knowing constancy is insight. Not knowing constancy leads to disaster. Knowing constancy, the mind is open. With an open mind, you will be open hearted. Being openhearted, you will act royally. Being royal, you will attain the divine. Being divine, you will be at one with the Tao. Being at one with the Tao is eternal. And though the body dies, the Tao will never pass away." - Chapter 16 of the *Tao Te Ching*

Fu can be interpreted in two ways: returning and reversing.

RETURNING TO THE TAO:

Since everything arises from the Tao, everything must return to the Tao. *Fu* means coming back to original nature (See *P'u* under "The Philosophy of Taoism – Ethics"). There, no personal action is necessary (*wu-wei* or non-doing) because the flow is in accordance with *ch'ang* (laws) (See "The Philosophy of Taoism – Metaphysics"). There is unchanging stillness and harmony with nature. Returning to one's source of sustained quietness and tranquility is the goal of Taoist meditation, and is synonymous with their concept of enlightenment.

REVERSING CYCLICAL MOVEMENT:

Changing directions is the second meaning of *fu*. This is the dynamic of the *I Ching* or *Book of Changes*. Everything cycles in *yin-yang* (See "The Philosophy of Taoism – Metaphysics") fashion. When *yin* reaches a maximum, it reverses and begins to diminish. *Yang* begins to ascend, reaches a maximum, and it too then reverses and so on.

We can easily understand this if we simply look at how we live and breath. We are active (*yang*) during the day, but then must return to rest (*yin*) at night. We breathe in (*yang*), and then return the breath out (*yin*).

The seasons arise, reverse, and return. What can continually increase without limit? Perhaps even the universe itself experiences immense cycles of expansion and contraction on the grandest of scales.

LIFE AND DEATH:

So here is the great question: Will our death be the first and only manifestation of *fu*? When we die, will we return to, and remain with the Tao, or will we be reborn again and again?

PRESCRIPTIONS:

NOTICE:

Notice how out of sorts you feel when you are thinking or acting in a manner inconsistent with your fundamental nature and your authentic self. You can tell when you are misaligned because of the tension you feel resulting from *cognitive dissonance.*

CORRECT:

Use the concept of *fu* to reverse any inappropriate direction. No matter how far down the wrong road you might travel, the minute you realize that you are off course, correct yourself immediately. Reverse direction, and get back on the right course. This course may not be a physical one. It could be one of thoughts, words, or actions. Apologize if necessary. A major fallacy people make is to say: *"Oh well, I've gone this far. I might as well continue."* Big mistake.

RETURN:

Sense the right path in your life, and return to it. Imagine the flow the Tao. Return (*fu*) to its *ch'ang* laws and its *chi* energy. Flow with its *yin* and *yang* cycles. Transform (*I*) to your highest self.

(From the West: "*Human kind cannot bear very much reality.*" - T.S. Eliot)

WU (NON-BEING)

"Thirty spokes share the wheel's hub; it is the center hole that makes it useful. Cut doors and windows for a room; It is the holes which make it useful. Therefore profit comes from what is there; Usefulness from what is not there." – Chapter 11 of the *Tao Te Ching*

DESCRIPTIONS:

***Wu* means "non being" or emptiness.**

This important concept is achieved by being at one with the Tao. There is nothing left to be done. The senses are void. The mind is not engaged and therefore is most receptive to the truth. The emotions are calm and peaceful. There is no striving. No action is necessary.

Wu or non-being is what is valuable to Taoists. The lead-in quotation provides some explanation to this sort of backwards utility.

PRESCRIPTIONS:

Review the section on *wu-wei*. Experiment with the state of *wu*. Meditate! Dissolve all mental contaminations. Suspend your relentless efforts for a while. Quite striving. Rid yourself of artificialities. Relax. Tune into the Tao. See how effective you can be without great effort. This is the essence of economy.

(From the West: *"To do nothing is the most difficult thing in the world – the most difficult and the most intellectual."* – Oscar Wilde)

NATURE

"Man follows the earth. Earth follows heaven. Heaven follows the Tao. Tao follows what is natural." - Chapter 25 of the *Tao Te Ching*

DESCRIPTIONS:

NATURE AND THE TAO:

We cannot specifically equate the unfathomable mystery of the Tao to anything, but it is most closely associated to the wisdom, spirit, and flow of nature.

NATURE AND TAOISTS:

Tzu-jan (authentic living) is tied in with nature. It means that the Taoist recognizes, respects, studies, and adopts the ways of nature. She is true to her self.

Tzu-jan also means leaving behind all that is unnatural. This includes the formalities of organized religions – the man-made rules, policies, conventions, rituals, myths, worship, sacrifices, and bureaucracy. To the Taoist, these are superfluous, digressive, and dispensable.

Taoists great perception of, and reverence for, the natural world, inevitably leads them away from the maddening crowd to a healthier place. He is intuitive, spontaneous, flexible, and adaptive. He harmonizes his internal energy with the coherent patterns of nature, balances the dynamic fluctuations of *yin* and *yang*, and flows with the cycles of his world - especially the seasons. He does not feel that nature's way is somehow incomplete and in need of human intervention. Mark Twain agreed when he said: *Architects cannot teach nature anything.* Taoists manifest their beliefs in their ecologically symbiotic and sustainable lifestyle.

NATURAL FOOD:

One mundane aspect of Taoist life that illustrates

their reverence for the natural order is in their relationship with food. Nature-loving Taoists eat seasonal, local, fresh, unadulterated food containing healthy active *chi* in balanced amounts of *yin* and *yang* energy. She eats to live rather than lives to eat, and recognize when she has had enough. Out of respect for herself, others, and the environment, she does not over consume or waste food. She is mindful of the needs of her contemporaries and of future generations. She never decimates any plant or animal specie, and plants for others in the future.

(From the West: "*In Aristotle, the conception of human nature is perfectly sound; every ideal has a natural basis, and everything natural has an ideal development*" – Santayana.)

PRESCRIPTIONS:

"The point we emphasize is strong confidence in our original nature." – Shunryu Suzuki

IN GENERAL:

Recognize and respect natural laws. There is infinite wisdom in the catechism of nature. Learn all the laws of science that you possibly can. Observe nature first hand. Witness the wonder of life. Ask yourself how a blade or grass defies gravity to move up toward the sun.

Study the subject of nature in both Eastern and Western philosophy.

RESPECT THE NATURE OF YOUR MIND:

Start by watching your mind. Control the monkey that swings from thought to thought. Let go of all thoughts that are unnatural, unhelpful, and unhealthy be they religious or secular.

We are endowed with two brain hemispheres for a reason. Each performs its own important function. Explore, develop, and use both. Tune into your holographic, feeling-based, intuitive, right brain hemisphere. Listen to the your linear, word-based, logical left side. Give both veto power over ideas i.e., if either one says "No" to a course of action, do not do it. Only consider moving forward with an idea if and only if both your intuitive and rationalistic sides agree.

RESPECT THE NATURE OF YOUR BODY:

Introduction:

Harmonize with nature by respecting the natural wisdom of your body. Your body is your interface with both the inner and outer world. It both sends and receives signals on both internal and external sensations. Pay attention to what it is telling you.

Be in your body.

Inside Example:

Instead of eating when everyone else does, how about eating when you are hungry, and abstaining when you are not? Fat is stored energy. When you take in more calories than you need, the excess energy is stored as fat. Avoid this input/output imbalance by sensing the nature of your own metabolic needs. Match input to output to prevent fat accumulation. If you want to loose fat, consume fewer calories than you are burning and your body will default to its stored energy.

Outside Example:

Always be mindful of environmental toxins. They include both people and things. Either resolve or depart from people and social situations that are harmful to you.

Avoid environmental threats to your health such as stress, air and water pollution, noise, chemicals, EMI, radon, etc. Why put yourself at risk? Some estimates indicate that occupational and environmental chemicals cause 70% of all cancers. Protect your body.

RESPECT THE NATURE OF YOUR EMOTIONS:

Remember once again the simple but powerful fact that you control your mind, and your mind controls your feelings. Therefore you control your feelings. Respect the nature of your emotions. If you do not like your current emotional state, ask what you have been thinking that created that state. You can always trace a negative state of mind back to a negative thought. Examine and manage the internal link between thought and feeling.

(From the West: "*Come forth into the light of things. Let nature be your teacher.*" – William Wordsworth)

WHOLENESS

"*Heaven's net is wide. Though its meshes are coarse, nothing slips through.*" – Chapter 73 of the *Tao Te Ching*

DESCRIPTIONS:

INTRODUCTION:

Taoism has the quantitative virtue of wholeness, discussed in this section, and the qualitative virtue of oneness, covered in the next section.

Since the Tao is limitless - without spatial

restrictions - Taoist perspective is limitless as well.

While maintaining a peaceful simplicity, Taoists are open to all the essential patterns in the intricate tapestry of life.

This quantitative inclusiveness is what is meant as "wholeness."

Wholeness is the comprehensive recognition of the totality of things. It is a spacious view of the panorama of life. It leaves nothing fundamental out. Wholeness focuses on the mental, physical, emotional, and spiritual dimensions of the "self." Wholeness also recognizes the abundance and necessity of the material world. Taoists know better than to assign "good" or "bad" labels on wealth, possessions, or resources. These things are viewed as morally neutral. They become effective ("good") or ineffective ("bad") in the way they are viewed and used. The basis of morality lies not in inanimate things, but with the intentions held by the people who use them.

CONNECTIVITY:

Wholeness inevitably leads the Taoist to connectivity. This idea asserts that everything is connected however remotely to everything else. We are aware of the obvious examples, and can infer the less obvious ones.

Quantum physics, string and membrane theory are postulating some very fascinating notions about connectivity. Here the Tao animates ripples along the marvelous, wondrous fabric of existence.

"LAW OF UNINTENDED CONSEQUENCES":

In embracing wholeness, Taoism inherently recognizes and respects the "Law of Unintended Consequences."

This law asserts that our thoughts, words, and actions often create unanticipated effects. In the West, this law is contained in *Chaos Theory* and *Complexity Theory*. These theories hold that interacting natural systems are extremely difficult to predict, and often generate unforeseen results.

PRESCRIPTIONS:

END MYOPIA AND GAIN PERSPECTIVE:

As you proceed through your day, especially when you begin to lose perspective and become unsettled, take a moment to regain your sense of wholeness. Break out of a narrow, overly schematic, monochromatic way of looking at things. Become aware of the totality of life. Be willing to experience every aspect of your potentials, even those parts that are most protected from pain. Recognize the rich diversity of your life; all the intellectual, physical, emotional, spiritual, financial, social, and environmental dimensions. View each as important and valuable. Get and stay in tune with them all. Once again as you did as a child, appreciate the little things. And then recognize the incomprehensible vastness of the world. Begin to view the world on a Wagnerian scale.

ONENESS

"Therefore wise men embrace the one and set an example to all." - Lao Tzu

DESCRIPTIONS:

INTRODUCTION:

Distinctions:

Wholeness is quantitative. Oneness is qualitative. Wholeness is the comprehensive recognition of the totality of things. Oneness is the comprehensive recognition of the unity of things.

Inconguency:

Who among us is personally, professionally, and socially unified? Most of us are a mosaic of contradictions. We think one thing, and say another. We present ourselves one way, and feel another. Our thoughts, words, and actions lack congruency. We are often unaware of our self-canceling vacillation. However, people around us often subconsciously, develop a healthy skepticism regarding our personal congruency.

Taoist Oneness:

Taoists first find unity inside - with their mind, body, and emotions or spirit. They then find unity outside – with all living things. This does not mean relinquishing personal responsibility or forgetting a healthy detachment. It does mean seeking that joy of affinity when the self is no longer at war with the other. Above all, Taoists return to the origin of all things – the Tao – where they find the ultimate oneness. (See the earlier section on *"Fu"*).

Types of Oneness:

Many spiritual traditions emphasize *oneness*. Here, we will examine four types of oneness, proceeding from the inside out:

- Oneness in thinking (non-dualism)
- Oneness within the self
- Oneness with others
- Oneness with the Tao

ONENESS IN THINKING - NON-DUALISM:

Non-Dualism:

Non-duality (See "The Psychology of Taoism") is seeing things without artificial differences and arbitrary boundaries. It is knowing what is meant by the concepts of impermanence, dependency, and undefinability, and then relating them to emptiness.

Non-dualistic thinking is seeing that the relativity and subjectivity of our opinions. Light and dark, up and down, long and short, hot and cold, etc. are all subjective opinions of phenomena on their continuums of existence. Our comments about them reflect a subjectivity; a judgment that belies our limited perspective.

Death: A Different Interpretation:

Chuang Tzu extended the concept of oneness to life and death. He viewed them both as stages in the same continuous process of change and transformation. This perspective can help overcome the fear of death.

Western Dualism:

Westerners have a penchant for breaking things into little pieces; for separating the parts from each other, and from the whole; and for treating each as a foreign, autonomous entity. We dissect a frog in biology class and think we are studying *life*. Just as we could not, without context, infer "whole wheat bread" from examining one of its ingredients such as grain, we cannot infer the ultimate development and purpose of many phenomena by examining their individual elements. It is only when things are visualized or witnessed in their temporal and spatial oneness that we are able to understand the full power of their potentials and the stages of multiplicity of their manifestations.

Saint Anthony had an interesting take on oneness. He believed that monks reached perfection when they no longer recognized themselves or what they were doing when they prayed. This is similar to the Buddhist concept of *samadhi*, or contemplative absorption.

ONENESS IN THE SELF:

Oneness in the self means that we are not in conflicted. We are one with our self as integrated, coordinated, and unified human beings. Our mind, body, and emotions are working together in an efficient, effective way. They are on the same page. The different systems and subsystems of our being are synergistic. Wherever we are on the spiritual path, we are internally harmonious at that stage of development.

ONENESS WITH OTHERS:

Oneness with others means that we reconcile and eliminate duplicitous behavior. It means that we have the humility to recognize our dependency on others. It means that we understand that we are all made of the same nuclear material, and have many of the same needs, desires, fears, and foibles.

Above all, oneness with others means that we can see our mutuality of spirit. We share the same divine light within. The essence of this connection with others is compassion. When we spontaneously generate compassion for others, we have truly internalized this form of oneness.

That said, oneness with others does not mean that we abandon the self or our sacred principles and ideals. It does not mean that we must like or even get along with everyone. There are always differences in style that are not "right" or "wrong", but just different tastes. We must retain our individuality, capacity for discretion, and right to accept or reject others and their behavior. To conform to, or even get along with, everyone would mean that we are malleable to an extreme. It would mean that we have little individuality or strength of principles. We are vulnerable to the conflicts of incompatibility, or worse, to the damage of hostility.

ONENESS WITH THE TAO:

Fundamentals:

The fundamental assumption in Taoism is the spiritual oneness of the material universe conceived as the unnamable and unknowable Tao. The goal is to be completely in harmony with it. This is not unlike others traditions emphasis of being at one with God, *Yahweh*, Allah, *Brahman*, *Kami*, great intelligence, higher power, or simply *The One*.

The Approach:

Oneness with the Tao is to be in accord with the ultimate reality that lies beneath everything. It cannot be fully comprehended or even directly known. It is approached by intuition and observation of ordinary experience. The goal of all life is to become unified with the wisdom, beauty, and power of nature's reality.

The following saying expresses this belonging and wholeness: *"The one in the many and the many in the one."* Fully understood and esteemed, this metaphysical mutuality can bring a calming and enlightening personal transcendence.

The Good News:

Here is the good news: The Tao is within all of us. Our metaphysical union with the Tao brings us in contact with immortality.

PRESCRIPTIONS:

IN GENERAL:

Seek oneness by replacing egocentrism with altruism; conflict with cooperation; criticism with compassion; differences with understanding; separateness with unity; and boundaries with continuum.

QUESTION DUALISTIC THINKING:

Consider the way you might view things as categorically different. Be careful how you analyze, separate, label, compartmentalize, and classify things. Question the way you separate things. Look for commonalities before you dichotomize, and break everything into this and that. Are the extremes real or just other points on a much broader spectrum? Above all ask if things are constitutionally different or rather a matter of degree different.

ONENESS WITH SELF:

Are you personally unified? Are your mind, body, and emotions congruent? Do they play as though they are on the same team or are they competing? Do they harmonize or are they out of tune with one another? Are they pulling together or are they going in different directions?

Here are some more specific questions that develop the point: Are you holding on to a belief so strongly that you are blocking out facts to the contrary? Is your spirit willing and your flesh weak? Is your mind saying one thing and your gut feelings saying another?

If the above questions have uncovered a lack of oneness of any type in you, identify and resolve all of your internal conflicts. Unite the diverse strands of your being into a splendid tapestry. Reunify yourself. Become personally congruent. Find personal oneness.

ONENESS WITH OTHERS:

Avoid wasteful conflicts with others. Instead of making enemies over differences that often do not matter, look for what you do share in common. Find areas of affinity with individuals in particular, and with humanity in general. Others are like you. They are struggling to understand and survive in the cosmic stream of time and space. We are all fellow travelers, each on our own sacred path with its own peaks and valleys. We must respect each other's journey.

JUDGMENT:

We often hear the cliché: *"Don't judge."* This is absurd. We were given the faculty of judgment and we use it every day in many ways. We judge all the time. If we did not, we would soon loose our capacity for discretion. We would eventually jeopardize our personal safety and economic well-being. Here is the important distinction that is often lost in the rush to not judge:

You cannot judge people in the high moral sense. No one knows all the hidden internal complexities of another's journey through life. However, you can and should judge how people fit and do not fit with you.

First, *Know thyself* – the famous Socratic dictum - then learn about others, and decide if there is a basis for sharing. Some people will be anathama to you. Avoid them all together. Others are non-toxic, but have different styles or are moving in different directions. Let them go their way. Keep your style if it works for you and maintain your course with a steady hand at the tiller. Some people will present an opportunity for personal or business synergy. Carefully decide if it is worthwhile. If so, compute the type and degree of interaction. Remember this important point:

In general, if you are going to err on one side of imbalance or the other, sharing too little is less damaging than sharing too much.

Always remember that it is easier to stay out, than to get out of both personal and professional entanglements.

ONENESS WITH THE COSMOS:

Seek an outer oneness. Develop a more enlightened understanding and overall vision of the outer world. Everyone and everything at any moment is the current result of an infinite number of antecedent events leading up to the present state of evolution. It is impossible to understand exactly how the infinite chain of *karmic* cause and effect has created the present condition. Do not expect the world to be any different than it is. You cannot change the past. Accept what is, then work to make everything better in the future.

See that you are a part of a great cosmic drama in the vast stream of matter and energy in time and space. Understand that everything in this stream connects in some way, however distant, to everything else. Become one with the eternal laws and truths that animate the universe (the Tao).

In general, seek an intelligent and balanced relationship with people, places and things. Replace criticisms with compliments, and watch doors open to you everywhere. End the warfare with the world, and flow with the laws of nature. In time, you may even begin to feel a peaceful Taoist unity with all living things.

(From the West: *"That is happiness: to be dissolved in something complete and great."* – Willa Cather)

DIVINATION

"The world is its own magic." – Shunryu Suzuki

DESCRIPTIONS:

INTRODUCTION:

One of the foundation books of Taoism is the *I Ching* or *Book of Changes*. One of its lasting and mysterious qualities is that it is oracular. We touched upon this divination aspect of the *I Ching* during the introduction. Here we will explore it in depth.

Many Taoists and non-Taoists believe that the oracle of the *I Ching* works though natural laws.

As we learned earlier in "The Philosophy of Taoism – Metaphysics", *yin* and *yang* are the two polar forces that continually interact with each other to create the 10,000 things. *Yin* and *yang* invariably cycle. Each takes turns becoming more and then less dominant with the other always present. This behavior, and the change (See *I* or change in the "Philosophy of Taoism – Metaphysics") they create, suggests predictability.

If a questioner has a clear mind and good heart, and asks a precisely worded question, the oracle will provide the appropriate answer, according to Taoist tradition.

WESTERN SKEPTICISM:

Westerners sometimes show skepticism and even ridicule toward the divination aspect of the *I Ching*. However, we should reconsider being parochial and dismissive about paranormal phenomena that we do not understand. The fact is that for over two millennia a large portion of the world's population have relied on the *I Ching for* guidance in daily living, for making business decisions, and for the governance of states.

SCIENTIST ADVOCATES:

Complimentary testimonials about the *I Ching* abound, some from prestigious sources. Two Chinese and one Japanese Nobel Prize physicists stated that they regularly consulted the oracle in various phases of their research. Perhaps they instinctively knew that something was happening at the subatomic level that could serve them well. (See "Synchronicity" below.)

THREE THEORIES:

I offer the reader three theories, which are not mutually exclusive, that might help to explain the oracular power of the *I Ching*.

THEORY-1: PSYCHOLOGICAL PROJECTION:

The first and most simple theory comes from the field of psychology. It is the human tendency to "project." We "project" our conscious and subconscious thoughts and feelings onto things. This is the principle behind the classic Rorschach inkblot test where subjects offer their interpretation of meaningless inkblots.

In other words, what we read into things is a reflection of our psychic state – our own beliefs, understandings, conditioning, needs, desires, fears, and personal experiences. And we may even be manifesting that which is hidden in the Freudian / Jungian world of the subconscious.

THEORY-2: SELF-FULFILLING PROPHECY:

A second theory to explain why a prediction from the *I Ching* could come true is that we make it come true. We tend to create what we expect (or suspect). The self-fulfilling prophecy has many ways of expressing itself. One of the most dramatic is the *placebo* effect. When test subjects are told that a drug produces a certain effect, the subject's body reacts as though that happened, even though the "drug" was actually an inert substance.

ADVENTURES IN DIVINATION
THE STORY OF A MASTERS COMMENTS

I once asked a seasoned Chinese *Tai Chi* master if the *I Ching* really had the power to forecast the future. He said it does - if you believe it does, and does not - if you do not. How people interact with these hexagrams to read, and perhaps shape, their future is personal and variable. There are no standard answers or predetermined destinies.

THEORY-3: SYNCHRONICITY:

A Crash Course in Synchronicity:

The third and most difficult to understand explanation of the *I Ching's* divination power is the esoteric idea of synchronicity. The famous Zurich psychoanalyst Dr. Carl Gustav Jung (1875-1961) studied the *I Ching* extensively. He believed that the oracular power of the text is based on what he called the *principle of synchronicity* or *meaningful coincidence*. He set forth this dramatic idea in his essay "*Synchronicity: An Acausal* (Not cause and effect) *Connecting Principle.*"

According to Jung, the following two factors coincide in synchronicity: An image arises in the conscious from the unconscious, and, at the same time, there manifests an event in the physical world that corresponds to that image.

A very simplistic explanation of synchronicity is that some events that are ostensibly "accidental" or "coincidental" are not. They are brought about, (in Jung's words) by a *"universal factor" and "a pattern that exists from all eternity, repeats itself sporadically, and is not derivable from any known antecedents."* It is *"partly the sum of countless individual acts of creation occurring in time."*

Jung's Great *Quaternio*:

So fundamental is synchronicity in Jung's cosmology that he elevates it to a level with three other universals to form his great *quaternio*, which follows:

- Space-Time Continuum
- Indestructible Energy
- Constant Connection through Effect (Causality)
- Inconstant Connection through Contingence, Equivalence, or Meaning (Synchronicity)

A Quantum Connection?

Has science discovered the same phenomena of synchronicity in the quantum physics laboratory? In their laboratory experiments, quantum physicists have observed certain phenomena at the subatomic level that may hold a clue to understanding synchronicity and in turn, the predictive powers of the *I Ching*. Strangely, they found that the mental states of the scientists conducting tests seem to inexplicably influence their physical outcomes.

This phenomenon might be related to Heisenberg's uncertainty principle, which states that any attempt at measurement must necessary disturb and alter what is being measured. Using the same seemingly magic subatomic interactions could our conscious, subconscious, unconscious, or even super conscious mind influence the outcomes of the *I Ching* divination process?

PRESCRIPTIONS:

GENERAL:

Keep an open mind. Get a book on the *I Ching* written by an authority. Ensure you are in a calm state of mind, and have a pure heart. Focus on a sincere question. Roll the coins. Build your two hexagrams following the steps below. Refer to the *I Ching* for the answers. See if they make sense to you. As time goes by, go back and see if they were accurate. This is fun, and can be quite rewarding. It makes a great parlor game with your friends.

THE PROCESS:

Here are seven basic steps for using the *I Ching* as an oracle:

Step-1:

Find a good version of the *I Ching*.

Step-2:

With a peaceful mind, and a good heart, ask a question and hold it in your mind. Your question can be about love, marriage, family, children, health, employment, business, investments, travel, etc.

Step-3:

Develop the first of two hexagrams. Use any three objects that can randomly provide one of two outcomes that represent *yin* and *yang*. In this process, *yin* has been assigned a value of two; *yang* a value of three. One of the most convenient methods to generate a hexagram is to simply toss three of the same type of coin. Tails can arbitrarily be designated *yin* (value 2), and heads *yang* (value 3). A three-coin toss can yield the following four possible results:

Coin Toss Results	Summed Values	Type of Line	Line Symbol
Three heads	3 + 3 + 3 = 9	Old *yang* line changing to young *yin*	---- O ----
Two heads, one tail	3 + 3 + 2 = 8	Young *yin* line unchanging	----- -----
Two tails, one head	2 + 2 + 3 = 7	Young *yang* line unchanging	------------
Three tails	2 + 2 + 2 = 6	Old *yin* line changing to *yang*	---- X ----

By tossing three coins six times, and layering the lines *from the bottom up,* you can develop a hexagram.

> Note: While the changing lines 9 and 6 above are indicated with the "O" and "X" for the purpose of development, they are indicated by regular *yang* (solid line) and regular *yin* (broken line) symbols respectively in the formation of trigrams and hexagrams.

Step-4:

Consult the *I Ching* for a *general* description of what this first hexagram means *in the present*. Study this description to determine what it means in your present personal life. You are the only one who can make this translation.

Step-5:

Next, develop a second hexagram by converting any *changing* lines in the first hexagram into what they would be if they already changed. Old *yang* lines (value 9) change into young *yin* lines (value 8). Old *yin* lines (value 6) change into young *yang* lines (value 7).

Step-6:

Again consult the *I Ching* for a general description of what this second hexagram means *in the future*. Study this description to determine what it means in your future personal life. Once more, you are the only one who can make this translation.

Step-7:

As time moves on, check to see if events are unfolding as predicted. You might be surprised at the *meaningful coincidences*.

(From the West: "*Consulting the I Ching is just like having a conversation with a very wise old gentleman.*" - Alan Watts)

PARADOX AND MYSTICISM

"Knock and He'll open the door. Vanish, and He'll make you shine like the sun. Fall, and He'll raise you to the heavens. Become nothing, and He'll turn you into everything." - Rumi

DESCRIPTION:

THE ENIGMAS OF TAOISM:

Laotsean and Chuangtsean Taoist philosophy is often paradoxical and mystical.

Examples: The Tao is the best way to live, but that way is a mystery. We must seek it, but it cannot be directly found. It is both the way the world is, and the way the world should be.

CYCLES:

There are ways to interpret these incomprehensibles. One way is to think in terms of cycles and the universal reversion to opposites (*yin-yang*).

For instance, we can begin to grasp the meaning behind the following two enigmatic statements from the *Tao Te Ching* by putting them in the context of cycles:

"If you want to be whole, let yourself be partial." - Chapter 22

"If you want to shrink something, first allow it to expand." - Chapter 36

WU-WEI:

Another way to begin to understand the teachings is

with the concept of *wu-wei* or non-doing. Basically, if we just leave things alone when they are proceeding according to their nature (the Tao), all will be well.

We can interpret the below mysterious statement from the *Tao Te Ching* by remembering the principle of *wu-wei* or not forcing:

"The best walking leaves no tracks. The best speech is flawless. The best calculation needs no counting slips. The best latch has no bolt, yet cannot be opened. The best knot uses no rope, yet cannot be untied." - Chapter 27 of the *Tao Te Ching*

"The Tao never does anything, yet through it all things are done." - Chapter 37 of the *Tao Te Ching*

"The Tao of heaven does not strive, and yet it overcomes. It does not speak, and yet is answered. It does not ask, yet is supplied with all its needs. It seems at ease, and yet if follows a plan." - Chapter 73 of the *Tao Te Ching*

MYSTERY:

All things are contained in the cosmic void of time and space - all spiritual and physical phenomena, all forces and energy, and all possibilities. Taoists develop a relationship with this void, but still consider its origin and that of all existence an incomprehensible mystery. (Buddha had the same view, and simply declined to speculate on unknowable metaphysical questions.)

PRESCRIPTIONS:

Study the descriptions in this book. Then read the *Tao Te Ching*. Analyze its profound and timeless wisdom in the context of the descriptions. When you have walked farther down your path in life, read it again and it will have new meaning.

Read the *I Ching*. Enjoy its art. Experiment with the oracle. Look in its vast ocean. See your soul's reflection.

(From the West: *"It's taken me all my life to understand that it is not necessary to understand everything."* - Rene Coty)

ENVOI

AS OUR PATHS PART:

If you are seeking a naturalistic approach to inner peace and beautiful living, then Taoism may be your answer. So as our paths part, I leave you with a final description and prescription:

DESCRIPTION:

The Tao is a vast and powerful stream in time and space. Each of us evolves from it, lives within it, and returns to it. Like little fish, we dart about in its vast currents. We can struggle against its power, and exhausted ourselves. Or, we can flow with its natural course, and travel far.

Taoism is about the intelligent choice.

PRESCRIPTION:

Can we capture the essential message of Taoism in a few words? Any attempt to do so would be futile.

Learn from nature.

GLOSSARY

Ch'ang: the unchanging, eternal, universal laws of the Tao

Feng Shui: the science and art of optimizing the flow of *chi* or energy

Fu: the Taoist concept of the return of all things to their source (the Tao)

Geomancy: that branch of classical cosmology, which studies the optimum harmony of man-made structures with the elements of the natural environment; a fundamental aspect of *Feng Shui*

I: Taoist term for change as in *I Ching, The Book of Changes*

Li: the natural, informal order of things

Qi: the newer name for *chi* or universal energy

P'u: Taoist term for one's untainted, original, true, nature; our authentic being

San Pao: "Three Treasures" of Taoism; mercy or love, moderation or simplicity; modesty or patience

Shar: poison arrow; in *Feng Shui* any line, edge, object, or structure inside or outside that points at you or your dwelling – especially the front door; shars threaten disaster and can be a counter, wall, sidewalk, driveway, road, or corner of a neighboring building

Sha-Chi: any objects or structures that block the harmonious flow of energy; sharp, pointed *sha chi* are called "hidden arrows" or "secret arrows" because of the threatening way they point outward.

Shen: Taoist term for deities

Sui Generis: Latin for "self-generating" (included here as a fundamental characteristic of the Tao)

Tao: "the way"; nature; the truth; the absolute; the eternal, infinite, natural force of law that created and animates the universe

Te: (as in *Tao Te Ching*): virtue, power, or great character; the energy of the Tao

Tsu: "the *formal* order of things as described or recorded" (contrast with *li*, the natural, undescribed order of things)

Tzu-jan: Taoist concept of spontaneous nature; natural living in tune with the Tao; authentic living

Wan-wo: the "10,000 things"; Chinese for literally the universe or everything in the universe

Wu: Taoist term for non-being

Wu-tse: Non-law

Wu-wei: Taoist concept of non-action; least effort progress; unmotivated action; not forcing against the grain; the wisdom of leaving things alone when they are naturally working

Ying-ning: the calmness and harmony that comes with *wu-wei* (non-action) when thought and behavior blend into oneness with the Tao